INSIGHT POCKET GUIDE

BARBADOS

D0543976

APA PUBLICATIONS

Part of the Langenscheidt Publishing Group

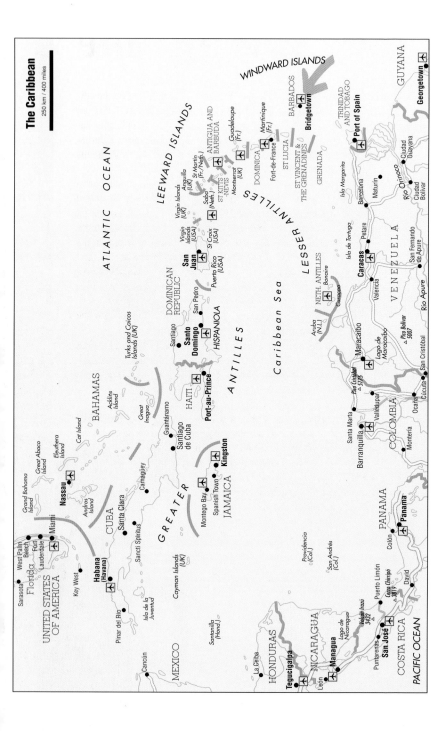

The Caribbean

250 km / 400 miles

Welcome

introduction

This is one of 133 itinerary-based Pocket Guides produced by the editors of Insight Guides, whose books have set the standard for visual travel guides since 1970. With top-quality photography and authoritative recommendations, this guidebook brings you the very best of Barbados in a series of tailor-made itineraries devised by Insight's Barbados correspondent, Roxan Kinas.

In these pages Barbados comes to life through a series of itineraries designed to show visitors the best of the island during a stay of about two weeks. Eleven itineraries, beginning with the capital Bridgetown on the west coast and then working around the island in a clockwise direction, link the chief attractions and beauty spots. Kinas pays due attention to the celebrated west coast, where royalty rubs shoulders with movie stars, and to the bustling and hip south coast, which has increased in popularity and developed over the years, but she also explores the island's quieter side, where donkey carts laden with fresh hay cluck slowly down narrow roads, where spectacular east coast beaches can be enjoyed in solitude, and the rugged landscape is breathtaking.

Supporting the itineraries are chapters on history and culture, shopping, eating out, nightlife and festivals, and a fact-packed practical information section that includes a varied selection of recommended hotels, apartments and beautiful tropical villas.

Roxan Kinas is a writer, natural life photographer and public relations consultant who has lived and worked on Barbados for more than 20 years. As well as writing for regional publications, such as *Maco Magazine, Caribbean Week* and *BWee Beat* (now *Caribbean Beat*), she produces feature articles about Barbados and the Eastern Caribbean islands for the North American press.

Pages 2/3: Bathsheba Beach
Pages 8/9: sunset at Carlisle Bay

History & Culture

When the British ship *William and John* landed at Holetown on February 17, 1627, no one was there to greet the 80 passengers who came ashore to settle and claim the island for England. Yet they were far from the first to land or even dwell on this wild and densely wooded island. Though the island lies just beyond the main trade and exploration routes of the time and had been bypassed by major explorers, many vessels had managed to stumble across it.

Long before that the south and west coasts were bustling with Amerindian life. Until recently it was assumed that the first inhabitants arrived from the Orinoco Valley around AD300. However, archaeological finds in the late 1990s, at sites such as Heywoods and Port St Charles, prove the island was a permanent settlement as early as 2000BC. The island's 75 archaeological sites suggest that Amerindian settlements existed up to AD1500, after which they disappeared. The reason for this is still unclear: the Amerindians could have been forced into slavery by the Spanish; wiped out by European diseases; or another tribe could have driven them from the island.

In the early 1500s Spanish and Portuguese ships prowled the region. Either by accident or design, ships from these nations passed through and mapped the island under several names, most notably Las Barbudos, which loosely translates as 'the bearded ones.' Whether these 'bearded ones' were trees (bearded fig) or people (bearded Amerindians) is speculation.

It was the British who settled the island and stayed. Barbados is unique in the region for having enjoyed a peaceful, unbroken relationship with its colonial parent until its independence on November 30, 1966. The island also has the oldest parliamentary system after Britain and Bermuda in the Commonwealth of Nations. British influence peppers the island in village names, etiquette, and lifestyle, but it is marinated in a rich African heritage. The mingling of these two influences gives the island a character unlike any other.

The Road to Sugar

By 1629 the island population had ballooned to 1,800, but, thanks to drought and lawlessness, a period known as the 'Starving Time' set in. The island's unpopular governor, Henry Hawley, was replaced by Sir William Tuft, but Hawley returned to power soon after. When his draconian methods nearly lost him the post a second time, Hawley changed his hard-line approach and the result was the establishment of the House of Assembly in 1639.

Barbados soon enjoyed prosperity based on tobacco and cotton. The primary labor pool for this work was drawn from white indentured servants, derisively called 'Red Legs,' who had come from England, Ireland, and

Left: a 17th-century view of Bridgetown
Right: Amerindian sacred object to the deity 'Giver of Cassava'

Scotland to escape political persecution or imprisonment. Some were condemned criminals, but others were from the higher echelons of British society, exiled in Barbados for their political beliefs. The indentured period was usually five or seven years, after which they would be given a small sum of money or a piece of land to make a new start.

The beginning of the English Civil War in 1642 brought unexpected benefits to Barbados. The 'Mother Country' turned her attention away from the colonies, and Barbados began trading with the Dutch, who were to play a pivotal role in the island's development. The war also brought a more refined settler, who replicated the lifestyle and economic prosperity enjoyed in England. It was at this time that Barbados became known as 'Little England.'

When the quality of the island's tobacco failed to compete in the world market and the supply of white indentured servants began to dry up, Barbados turned to sugar. The first canes arrived from Brazil in 1637 and local planters began manufacturing sugar with the help of the Dutch, who supplied canes, mill technology and the West African slaves for this labor-intensive crop. It was soon discovered that a potent drink could be made from fermented molasses, a by-product in the sugar-making process. These were the crude beginnings of the rum industry that exists today.

The influx of cultured British settlers coupled with a vast new labor pool and a slow mastery of the art of sugar production ushered in a period of unprecedented prosperity. From 1651 until the early 1700s Barbados was said to be the most prosperous island of the British West Indies, and one of the most successful British colony islands in the world.

A new 'plantocracy' class reigned. Lavish plantations were designed after the popular Jacobean and Georgian styles (examples of which remain today), and the ruling class led an opulent, sometimes decadent lifestyle, with monumental homes and furnishings. Gambling was a favorite pastime that often lost an owner his entire plantation.

Top: a member of the 'plantocracy' relaxes
Left: a statue of Bussa, leader of a slave revolt

Slavery

By 1712 Barbados had close to 42,000 slaves. Despite the oppression and severe hardships, runaway and rebellious elements remained small compared with other islands. Several thwarted uprisings took place in the late 1600s, but on such a small island, almost completely planted with canes and other crops, there was nowhere to run.

However, by the end of the 18th century the combination of harsh conditions, the influx of replacement slaves less resigned to a life of unrelenting hardship, and the advent of 'free-colored people' (freed African slaves) added to a growing air of dissent. Outside Barbados the great reform movement was building, and after the British parliament's 1807 abolition of the slave trade freedom was on the horizon.

In 1816 free mulatto (an old-fashioned term used to describe a person of mixed racial parentage) Washington Francklyn masterminded a slave revolt. Among the leaders was the now famous Bussa, a headman at Bayley's Plantation. Cane fires set in St Philip signaled the start of the revolt and burned their way into neighboring parishes.

The slaves stood little chance against a regiment of local militia. In the end one-fifth of the island's crop was razed, property was destroyed, 176 enslaved people died fighting, and another 214 were executed, including Francklyn. Bussa died in battle. It took another 22 years of stubborn resistance by the planters, however, before slavery was finally abolished in 1838.

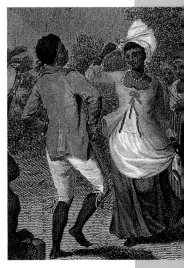

Though imported slaves came primarily from West Africa, language barriers and diverse cultural backgrounds made it difficult for them to carry on their traditions on Barbados. Among the elements of African culture that did survive the centuries are a belief in *obeah*, or magic, a smattering of words, and distinct African influences in diet and music.

Riots, Reforms, and Independence

By the start of the 20th century, Barbados was feeling the crush of an ever increasing population, and the austere economic conditions that ensued, combined with the lack of union or constitutional representation of the general labor force, led to riots. On July 26, 1937 workers amassed in Bridgetown for a meeting to discuss the deportation of Trinidadian union agitator Clement Payne. The situation escalated out of control, and soon Bridgetown was in a shambles. Rural areas quickly caught wind of the disorder and followed suit, resulting in 14 deaths, many injuries, hundreds of arrests and widespread damage to property.

The incident led to the launch, in 1938, of the Barbados Progressive League, later to become the Barbados Labour Party (BLP). Under the leadership of Oxford-educated barrister and journalist Grantley Adams (later knighted), the party had within two years of its formation won five parliamentary seats. Again under Adams' leadership, the Barbados Workers'

Right: a couple enjoy a dance

Union was formed, leading to a virtual revolution in employment and living conditions, as well as important constitutional and educational reforms.

A highly qualified professional, Sir Grantley came to be known as the leader of the island's 'social revolution,' working tirelessly to build the labor movement both at home and in the wider region. By 1958 the Cabinet system was instituted, with Adams becoming the island's first premier.

One of the Labour Party's members elected in 1951 was left-wing Errol Walton Barrow. After crossing swords with Grantley Adams over labor and other issues, Barrow broke away from the party and in 1955 formed the Democratic Labour Party (DLP). Later, in a stunning 1961 election victory, he became the nation's leader.

Errol Barrow, today a national hero, was responsible for leading Barbados to Independence in 1966. He introduced free education, launched the still-active school meals program, and significantly improved the wages and working conditions of public workers.

In 1976 a young upstart usurped Barrow in an overwhelming election defeat. The young leader was J. M. G. M (Tom) Adams, the son of the late Sir Grantley. But Barrow refused to give up, and he remained in politics, winning the election in 1986 and leading the nation until his death in June the following year.

Barrow was succeeded by Lloyd Erskine Sandiford, who enjoyed seven years in power. However, the nation grew increasingly disheartened in the face of a faltering economy. At the next election, in 1994, the Barbados Labour Party led by Owen Arthur, was returned, heralding a new period of optimism. His shrewd management restored faith in the economy and attracted significant foreign investment, ushering in a new era of prosperity.

Economic Development

Much of Barbados' modern-day prosperity is due to a flourishing tourism industry that dates back to the 1700s, when visitors came for the salubrious climate. In 1751 George Washington accompanied his tubercular brother Lawrence to the island, the only occasion he ever left his homeland. Later, in the first half of the 20th century, Barbados became a popular long-stay winter destination for wealthy British visitors, many of whom built lavish homes along the west coast. In the last 25 years of the 20th century visitor arrivals doubled, and today tourism is the island's primary revenue earner, bringing close to 500,000 visitors each year. The growth of the cruise ship industry has been a major contributing factor.

However, Barbados has not lost touch with its agricultural roots and its long tradition of sugar production. Although sugar has had its peaks and troughs over the years, in 2006 Barbados produced over 33,000 tons of sugar. The industry continues to face challenges such as competing demands for land, old machinery, and high labor costs, but for now it still generates

Left: farm workers on strike in the 1940s

significant foreign exchange. The farming sector also contributes to the island's financial success, with the most popular agricultural goods being root crops, fruits and vegetables, dairy products, chicken, and fish.

Barbados also has a healthy manufacturing industry that features mostly light industrial products such as cement blocks, clay tiles, paint, chemicals, and electronic components. There is also a thriving commercial sector, which includes international business and financial services, focusing on developing offshore business. A buoyant economy is often accompanied by a construction boom, and in Barbados this labor-intensive industry is helping to reduce unemployment levels. However, the government remains the biggest employer on the island.

Hard Times Celebrated

The island's biggest festival, Crop Over, traces its roots back to the plantation era, when the end of the harvest represented both the end of hard work and the start of hard times. It was a plantation event – a day for role reversal and frolic. As the last procession of carts made their way into the mill yard, a laborer would beat a makeshift gong, announcing the crop over.

The draft animals and carts were decorated with flowers and the canes themselves tied with bright bandanas. The workers joined the procession, all wearing flowers in their headgear. One cart would carry a cane effigy of 'Mr Harding' (symbolizing hard times and the cruel gang-drivers) which was burned at the end of the festivities. (The 'Mr Harding' element has been dropped from modern-day festivities.) After the parade around the yard, a speech was made by a favored worker, followed by a reply by the owner or manager. Festivities were then punctuated by lavish spreads of food and drink – usually rum – along with games and contests, including the now dying art of 'stick-licking' (stick fighting), dancing, and singing. Music was a key element.

These days an entire month of activities is devoted to the festival. Many original elements, such as the donkey cart parade and the ceremonial delivery of the last canes, remain in some form. Other elements, including calypso tents and competitions, evolved in the 1970s, when Crop Over (starting in July) was revived after a 30-year hiatus.

During the festival virtually every form of music the island has to offer is heard, including Tuk, a fusion of

Above: a cruise ship calls. **Right:** a Tuk band plays. **Over Page:** a chattel house

British marching music and African rhythms. Roving Tuk bands wend their way through the crowds playing the kettle drum, bass drum and penny whistle in a unique format and cadence, beginning with a slow waltz, moving into a marching rhythm, and concluding in a frenetic African beat.

The Chattel House

An historical aspect of Barbados still apparent today is the chattel house, the quaint, colorfully painted houses found in rows throughout the island.

Chattel means 'movable possession,' and the buildings originated when newly emancipated African slaves were required to provide their own housing while working on the plantations. They needed homes that could be taken apart, moved and reassembled all in one day. Such housing was located on plantation land in an area known as a 'tenantry,' where the soil level was too shallow for cultivation.

The houses were made from pine and were of fixed dimensions, such as 8 by 16ft (2.4 by 4.9m), 10 by 20ft (3 by 6m) or 9 by 12ft (2.7 by 3.7m), based on pre-cut lengths imported from North America. Each unit was divided into a minimum of nine sections: four sides, a floor, two gables, two roof sections, and interior partitions. While the original chattel houses looked similar to the ones built today, the early ones were in fact cruder, having first thatch, later shingles, and after the 1955 Hurricane Janet galvanized roofing.

Their construction was of mortise-and-tenon style, where frame and joints fitted into one another. This made the building stronger against the elements and more easily dismantled. It also allowed the owner to expand at the back and/or front as the family grew or came into more money.

The houses were set on coral stone blocks for easy moving and to give them added elevation for greater privacy, protection from flooding and better floorboard ventilation. This method of propping the houses is still seen island-wide. Always symmetrical in appearance, they had a front door in the center with a window to each side. Variety came in the type of doors and windows used, and the color.

The Tenantry Act of 1981 allowed chattel house owners to purchase the land on which they stood at a low rate. Subsequent to this, a more permanent bungalow-style house emerged, with cement foundations and walls.

The chattel house remains a beautiful and indigenous part of the culture, their riot of colors dotting the countryside with a distinctive flourish.

HISTORY HIGHLIGHTS

2000BC Barbados is discovered by Amerindians from the Orinoco Basin.

200BC Amerindians of the Saladoid period make the first permanent settlements along the south coast, Heywoods, Hillcrest, and Bathsheba.

AD800 New Amerindian settlements develop in the Troumassoid period.

1200 Amerindian population explosion with over 60 sites on the coast.

1500 The Spaniards land on Barbados; Amerindians are wiped out.

1536 A Portuguese ship lands and finds the island uninhabited.

1625 The first English ship, *The Olive*, stumbles onto Barbados, landing at what will become Holetown. They claim the island for James I of England.

1627 Barbados becomes an English possession with the landing of the *William and John* containing 80 settlers.

1628 Bridgetown is founded.

1637 The first sugar cane plants are imported from Brazil.

1639 The House of Assembly is established in Bridgetown.

1642 Sugar is manufactured for the first time, rum – produced from molasses – is discovered as a by-product.

1644 West African slaves arrive in vast numbers to support the island's new labor-intensive sugar industry.

1675 The first slave uprising is thwarted; 17 ringleaders are executed.

1766 Bridgetown is destroyed by fire.

1816 The 'Bussa' slave revolt results in considerable crop and property damage and the death of almost 400 slaves.

1831 Free colored people are granted legal equality with whites. The 'Great Hurricane' devastates the island.

1834 The Emancipation Act launches the apprenticeship system in anticipation of the emancipation of all slaves.

1838 Slavery is abolished.

1843 Samuel Jackman Prescod is the first black man elected to the House of Assembly.

1884 A Franchise Act lowers voter qualifications to people earning £50 a year.

1902 An outbreak of smallpox leads to death, quarantine, and isolation.

1924 Charles Duncan O'Neal sets up the Democratic League of Barbados.

1937 Labor riots, sparked by harsh economic conditions, break out.

1938 The Barbados Progressive League (later the Barbados Labour Party, BLP) is set up, led by Grantley Adams.

1954 Grantley Adams becomes the island's first premier.

1955 Cricketer Garfield 'Gary' Sobers sets the world record for the most runs in a test match, scoring 356 not out.

1961 The Democratic Labour Party (DLP) wins its first election under the leadership of Errol Barrow.

1966 Barbados becomes an independent nation.

1974 The sugar crop festival, Crop Over, is revived.

1976 The BLP wins the election and Tom Adams is appointed Prime Minister. Billie Miller becomes the first woman to serve in the Cabinet.

1979 The airport opens, with a long runway to accommodate Concorde.

1989 Barbados celebrates 350 years of unbroken parliamentary rule.

1996 Barbados and other Caribbean community (Caricom) nations renew debate on the launch of a Caribbean Court of Appeal to replace the existing appeal system of the British Privy Council (Judicial Committee).

1997 August 1 is designated Emancipation Day, a national public holiday.

1998 Ten Barbadian National Heroes are announced.

1999 Trafalgar Square, Bridgetown is renamed National Heroes Square.
The BLP win elections, taking 26 seats.

2000 Sprinter Obadele Thompson wins a bronze medal at the Olympics.

2003 The BLP, led by Owen Arthur, win the election.

2004 Hurricane Ivan damages the cruise ship terminal and several homes.

2007 Barbados hosts the ICC Cricket World Cup final.

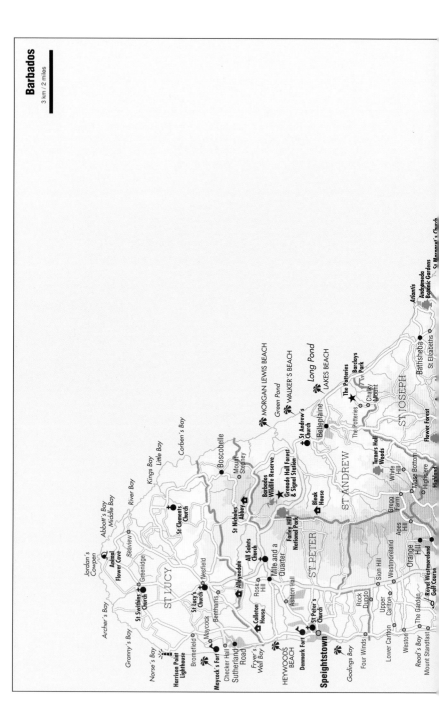

Barbados

3 km / 2 miles

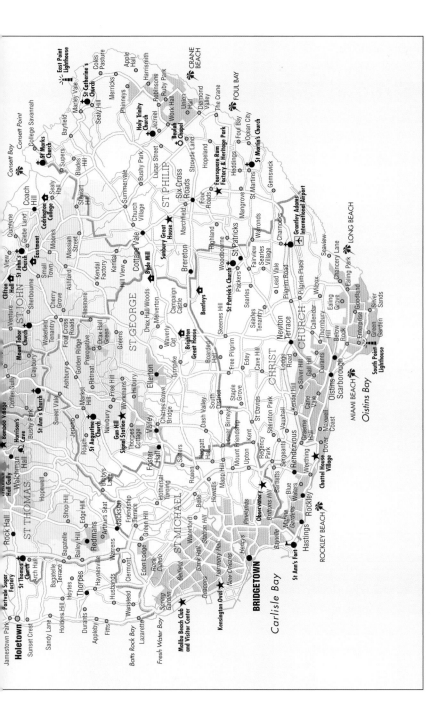

Orientation

Each of Barbados' 11 parishes offers something unique, something special. In the following itineraries the island has been divided into regions, loosely using the parishes as guidelines.

The northeast, southeast, and central itineraries include the main sights, ranging from historic buildings to specialty parks, while the south and west itineraries visit coasts, that are highly developed, with palm-fringed beaches and calm waters. Ideal for watersports, these areas also have some of the island's best shopping. Especially pleasing is a trip through the northern countryside, which offers scenic views of land that is peppered with parks, colorful gardens, and plantations; there is also a wildlife reserve. Also located in the north is Harrison's Cave, one of the island's most popular attractions. The tour of the capital Bridgetown reveals colonial landmarks, parliament buildings, bustling markets, art galleries, and waterfront cafés.

The interior landscape is lush with rolling hills and rich vegetation that provide more scenic views than the flatter coastal areas, but the latter offer an unsullied rugged beauty that is just as appealing.

In striking contrast to the interior, strong Atlantic waves crash over the cliffs and rough rocks on the east coast. The eastern tour takes in Bathsheba, plantation houses, historic sites and landmarks in the St George Valley, and country nature trails. What one person finds intriguing and worth a few hours' visit, another may consider less exciting. Therefore, many of the guide's trips include several diverse attractions and you can choose whichever interests you most, or pick and mix excursions based on the time you have to spare.

Getting Around

Though small, just 166 sq. miles (430 sq. km), Barbados has a veritable maze of unmarked winding roads. Do not get frustrated if you find yourself lost after mistaking a main road for a secondary one, or if you make a wrong turn. Just relax and consider it part of the fun of exploring the island. Most Barbadians are friendly and will, if asked politely, be happy to point you in the right direction.

We will be using the 'ABC' Highway as the starting point for the tours. This highway stretches from the airport to the edge of St James in the west. Here the road parts, extending either to the coast (ABC continuation) or inland on Highway 2A to the north and St Peter. The highway is interrupted by roundabouts, which will be used to start and end the tours. Once you have located the best route to get onto the 'ABC,' use that to begin your tours.

Several of the historic properties included in the itineraries are owned, operated, or supported by the the Barbados National Trust (BNT).

Left: Maycock's Beach
Right: a lifeguard keeps an eye on visitors

The Capital & Environs

1. BRIDGETOWN *(see map below)*

A morning walking tour of Bridgetown's historic sights. Lunch along the careenage and an afternoon shopping. If you plan to shop duty free don't forget your passport and ticket. Guard your belongings carefully while in the city.

For this tour you can take a bus or van into Bridgetown then walk around the sights. If you intend to drive and are arriving from the south coast, park near the heliport. West coast visitors enter Bridgetown from Spring Garden Highway then Fontabelle, and park in the city center car park, a block off Broad Street.

Bridgetown was established in 1628, but it was not the most favorable site to found a city, for the nearby sea and swamp guaranteed episodes of disease and flooding. Richard Ligon in his book *True & Exact History of Barbadoes* (1657) noted: 'A town ill situate; for if they had considered health, as they did conveniency, they would never have set it there…But, one house being set up, another was erected, and so a third, and a fourth, till at last it came to take the name of a Town.' Despite the flooding and poor sanitation, the town grew.

The capital's name is traditionally believed to come from a primitive Amerindian bridge spanning the waterway. Early deeds mention 'The Indian Bridge,' 'The Indian Bridgetown' and 'The Bridge.' By 1660, St Michael's Town became the favored name, and was in use into the 19th century. The

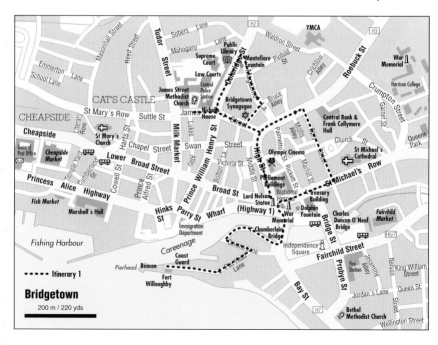

Bridgetown

200 m / 220 yds

· · · · Itinerary 1

main streets of Bridgetown were laid out by surveyor John Swan, and the street behind Broad Street was later named after him.

Broad Street (the main thoroughfare) was originally a market area called Cheapside, but today, only the far western end and the market are known by that name. In the late 1600s it was called the Exchange or Exchange Street because of the Merchants' Exchange there, but by the early 1700s it had become Broad Street.

At the top of Broad Street is **National Heroes Square**. Formerly known as Trafalgar Square, it features a **statue of Lord Nelson** erected in 1813 – some three decades before London's own Nelson's Column – although there are plans to move it to another location. Plans to raise a statue in Nelson's memory were begun within weeks of his victory and subsequent death at Cape Trafalgar in 1805. In fact, it was a tremendous source of pride to Barbadians, who thought they were the first (in fact they were the third, after Montreal and Birmingham) to raise a monument honoring the military leader. Sculpted from bronze by Sir Richard Westmacott ('the first castor of bronze in the Kingdom'), it is regarded as an excellent likeness of the British admiral.

The land occupied by National Heroes Square was first purchased in 1807 and expanded to its present size in 1826. The fountain, known as the **Dolphin Fountain**, was erected in 1865 to commemorate the advent of piped water in Bridgetown. The garden itself and the enclosure came slightly later, the earliest work beginning in 1882.

Parliament

Across from the statue in National Heroes Square are the Public Buildings, now called the **Parliament Buildings**. Plans to erect a parliament and public records building were initiated in 1692 after the island's new governor arrived to discover sessions were being held in public houses (taverns), but

the capital & environs

apart from a brief period (1700–1704) when meetings were conducted in the more appropriate State House they continued to be held in public houses, residences and other rented facilities until the Public Buildings were erected in 1871, almost 240 years after parliament was established in Barbados. It took a tragedy to spark action. After a devastating fire in 1860 the Public Buildings Erection Committee acquired plots from what was called the New Burnt District.

The first (West) building was completed in late 1871 and presented to government on January 1, 1872. The East building was completed in 1874, and in 1875 the clock and bells, imported from England, were installed in its tower. However, the weight of the tower and its contents was too heavy for the foundations and the building began to sink. In 1884 the clock was taken out and the south tower of the West building was redesigned to hold it. Made by B. R and T Moore, the eight-day Public Buildings clock even runs while being wound.

The Parliament Buildings are designed in neo-Gothic style, a 19th-century copy of medieval religious architecture. Of note are the stained-glass windows depicting all the British monarchs from James I to Queen Victoria, as well as Oliver Cromwell, the 17th-century Lord Protector. The West wing will house a gallery dedicated to the National Heroes of Barbados.

The Old Quarter

Walk up High Street (northern side of National Heroes Square) then turn onto James Street and walk one block to the tiny alleyway called Synagogue Lane on the right. As you come up this short street, you will see the **Syna-**

gogue (Mon–Fri 9am–4pm) on the site of the first Jewish synagogue in the Western hemisphere, built in 1654. That building was destroyed by the Great Hurricane of 1831 and the current one was opened in 1833.

By 1929 there was only one practicing Jew left in Barbados and the synagogue was sold and turned into offices. By the early 1980s the building was derelict and the local Jewish community launched a restoration effort with assistance from the Barbados National Trust, the government and the Caribbean Conservation Association.

Today the synagogue is in active use and has received various preservation awards and accolades. Next to the building is the **Jewish cemetery**, with graves dating back to 1660.

Synagogue Lane leads to Magazine Lane – so named because it was near the site of the Public Magazine, built in 1683 by Simon Cooper, then demolished in 1728 to make room for the Town Hall at the corner of James and Coleridge streets.

Turn left on Magazine Lane to view **Montefiore Fountain**, a drinking fountain presented to the City of Bridgetown in 1864 by Swan Street businessman John Montefiore in memory of his father, who died in 1854. The

Previous Page: Lord Nelson stands guard near the Parliament building; downtown street vendors. **Above:** the entrance to the Synagogue

father, also named John, was a prominent Bridgetown merchant described in historical archives as a 'free colored.' The fountain's first home was in another section of the city called Beckwith Place, at the corner of Broad and Tudor streets. It was moved to its present site in June 1940. Each side of the fountain is decorated with a marble mythical figure representing one of four attributes: Fortitude ('Look to the End'), Temperance ('Be soberminded'), Patience ('To bear is to conquer'), and Justice ('Do wrong to no one').

Across from the fountain is the **Public Library**, opened in 1904 and paid for by the Scottish-American philanthropist Andrew Carnegie. It stands on part of the land that was the prison yard of the Common Gaol. Climb the outside steps of the library and have a look at the beautiful room that houses the children's library. It retains its original ceiling, which has been restored.

Next door is a cluster of buildings, including the **Law Courts** and the **Supreme Court** building, formerly the Town Hall. This edifice was built in 1730 for housing the Legislature, Law Courts, and the Common Gaol. While the gaol primarily confined civil and criminal offenders, it occasionally served as a prisoner of war facility. Many prisoners were moved to Glendairy Prison on its completion in 1855, and the Town Hall Gaol was closed in 1876. Though the Law Courts section of the compound was altered in the 1950s with the addition of a verandah that leads from the Registrar's office to the Central Hall, you can still see the beauty of the building at its eastern end.

To reach **Nicholls House**, considered the oldest surviving building in Bridgetown, walk from the library past the island's first police station to James Street. Nicholls House is on the corner, on the same side of the street as the police station. Reflecting the Dutch influences introduced to Bridgetown during the 17th century, Nicholls House has classic Dutch gabling and an attic door in the center which originally housed a winch for hauling merchandise. The building, now a law office, was named after a father/son team of dentists who were based here from the 1930s for some two decades.

The next sight on the itinerary is St Michael's Cathedral. Go down James Street and turn left at the large junction to meet Roebuck Street. Follow it to Spry Street, just a block or so ahead on the right. You will see a tall, imposing modern building, which is

Top: St Mary's Church offers shelter in a storm
Right: a snow cone will cool you down in town

the **Tom Adams Financial Centre**, home to the Central Bank of Barbados and the Frank Collymore Hall, a cultural centre. Pass the Masonic Lodge, a large older building which was the first site of Harrison College, and **St Michael's Cathedral** (guided tours available) is on your left. This is the second Anglican church to be built on this site. The first, consecrated in 1665, was destroyed by a hurricane in 1780, but even before nature razed it, the building was nearly wrecked by incompetent repair work necessitated by the massive roof span. The new building was erected soon after the hurricane, but it too suffered structural problems. It became a cathedral in 1825 under William Coleridge, one of the West Indies' first Anglican bishops.

It is probably now time for lunch and a walk along the historic careenage. Continue on to St Michael's Row, turn right, and you will see the Fountain Gardens ahead. Go back to the top of Broad Street, cross the Chamberlain Bridge and turn right down the careenage walkway.

The Harbour

The **Chamberlain Bridge**, formerly known as the 'swing bridge,' was renamed after Joseph Chamberlain, the British Colonial Secretary in the late 1800s who was instrumental in salvaging a floundering sugar industry burdened by excessive taxation. In the early days a wooden bridge was built to replace the Indian bridge settlers found when they arrived. Several other versions were erected and subsequently destroyed, mostly by fire, flooding, or hurricane. One of many amusing bridge-building episodes occurred in 1751 after the government commissioned John McDonnell to construct a stone bridge in place of the constantly faltering wooden structures. On completion, the wooden scaffolding was dismantled and the bridge immediately collapsed, the stones all tumbling into the channel and blocking it. Having spent £3,595, only to have this albatross fail, the government prosecuted those involved. Built in 1872, the bridge no longer swings and is closed to traffic.

Walk the length of the careenage (so called because the old wooden ships

the capital & environs

would be 'careened' or turned on their sides to have their hulls cleaned here) and before the end you will come to the screw dock. Built between 1889 and 1893, this dry dock is a fine example of Victorian engineering and is thought to be the only dock of its kind in the world. An intricate piece of workmanship, it provided respite and repair for ships for almost a century.

On the careenage is the **Waterfront Café**, ideal for lunch with scenic views of the harbour. Or, if you fancy eating beachside walk a little further along Bay Street to the **Boatyard**.

If you need to work up an appetite the wharf is the place to arrange water-based activities such as deep-sea fishing, catamaran cruises and scuba diving. On the far shore or northern bank, **Bajan Helicopters** (tel: 431-0069) have exciting 20- and 30-minute flight-seeing tours.

Before you head back to town it's worth stopping for a spot of shopping along the careenage, where **Soul Philosophy** and **Colours of de Caribbean** sell clothing and souvenirs. On the site of the old Harbour Police station is Bayshore complex (near the Boatyard), which has a smart restaurant, public phones, changing facilities and showers, if you want to cool off in Carlisle Bay.

2. THE GARRISON   *(see map, page 28)*

A walking tour around the historic Garrison with a stop at the Barbados Museum. If you go on a Saturday morning, in season, you can attend the afternoon horse races at the Savannah.

The Garrison is on the southern outskirts of Bridgetown, just off Bay Street. You can get there from Bridgetown or follow Highway 7. From either direction, turn into Bush Hill (opposite the Barbados Light & Power Company building). At the first monument turn right and drive the few yards to the cannons. There is ample parking but come early if it is a race day.

This is an introductory tour around the Garrison. If you have a special interest in the history of Barbados, buy 'The Barbados Garrison and its Buildings' *(see page 91)*, which highlights all the buildings of the old Garrison in detail.

The Garrison buildings encircle the Savannah, which was originally the parade ground for the British troops stationed here. Today the Garrison Savannah is synonymous with horse racing; in fact the first horse race was held here in 1840. The grounds are maintained by the Barbados Turf Club which runs three race seasons a year: January to April; June to August and October to December (tel: 426-3980 for further information). The Savannah also attracts a large number of fitness enthusiasts, who train here in the evening. National ceremonies such as the Independence Day Parade (November 30) are held at the ground and at Easter time there is a kite flying competition.

Top left: inside St Michael's Cathedral.
Left: landing barracudas. **Right:** on shore leave

Military Might

There are 60 to 70 Garrison buildings in all. While many of these are now in private or government use, efforts are underway to bring some back to their original appearance, as well as to use the St Ann's Fort compound (now occupied by the Defense Force) to house collections of important artifacts, including the National Cannon Collection.

This was the first garrison in the Caribbean and probably predates any in North America too. Barbados had some 50 forts and batteries around the island and was well fortified from the 1600s, first by the Barbados militia, then by the British Army.

A litany of events caused the people of Barbados to feel the need for fortifications. The first was around 1650, when Needham's Fort (soon after renamed Charles Fort) was constructed at Needham's Point to stave off a landing by the Commonwealth Expedition under Oliver Cromwell's rule. Though the fort was originally made from branch bundles it apparently served them well, for it was action from here that fended off invasion by a Dutch fleet in 1665.

St Ann's Fort was built after war with France started in 1688. Originally intended to be a 'little castle or detached bastion' to support Fort Charles, St Ann's was ultimately built as a 1½-acre (0.6-ha) stone hexagon to the east of Fort Charles.

When France declared war on Britain in 1778 and took neighboring British West Indies possessions, the military picture changed profoundly and it appeared only a matter of time before Barbados would also be taken. England swiftly dispatched troops and naval forces to Barbados. By 1783, with the promise of more troops to come and the island unable to accommodate the great numbers already here, temporary barracks and facilities were built, but with the ending of the American Revolutionary War that same year the bulk of the British troops stationed on the island were withdrawn and sent elsewhere.

In 1785, to prevent any further threats to its West Indies territories, the British Government decided to establish permanent land forces in the Windwards and Leewards with Barbados as the headquarters. Construction of the British Garrison began in earnest in 1789 after the purchase of some 64 acres (26ha) of land. By the time construction of British facilities began, St Ann's Fort embraced some 14 acres (5.7ha), which were still under the domain of the Barbados Colony government. The first British buildings – the

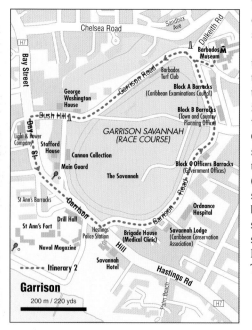

Garrison

200 m / 220 yds

Powder Magazine and Ordnance Storehouse – were built inside St Ann's *(see page 30)* walls, along with the Drill Hall barracks on the north side of the fort, even though the British Army did not merge St Ann's Fort into the Garrison until 1811. Fort Charles remained out of the loop until 1836. Various other buildings were constructed in the early 19th century, including the Commissariat Provision Store in 1801, which today serves as the Light & Power Company building.

When Britain's troubles with neighboring France recurred in the late 1700s (around the time of the French Revolution), Barbados became the springboard for military expeditions to nearby territories held by the enemy. Even though many Garrison buildings were up by this time, they proved woefully inadequate for the troop numbers that were moving through the island. This problem, compounded by further spats in the Napoleonic Wars in 1803, prompted swift construction of still more facilities.

A Changing Role

With each renewed military threat, more buildings sprang up, and the area soon consumed more than 150 acres (61ha). Construction continued at a rapid clip, even though the role of the Garrison changed with the times. As the wars with France abated, internal problems erupted. The slave revolt of 1816 was put down by the British regiment, and this event led to the establishment of a chain of signal stations manned by the Royal Artillery.

The 1831 Great Hurricane, which nearly flattened the whole island, severely damaged much of the Garrison, with one account reporting, 'almost every building on the Garrison was demolished.' But it was yellow fever more than anything else that made life miserable for the troops, with many dying from the mosquito-borne disease each year.

Troop numbers seemed to peak around 1815, with some 2,700 stationed at the Garrison. The last British troops left in November 1905, and in January 1906, the 1st West India Regiment withdrew, leaving a small number of officers behind to tie up loose ends. The Garrison functioned for 126 years as it was intended, leaving in its wake a legacy of buildings, artillery and artifacts.

Above: clock tower and cannon in front of the Main Guard. **Right:** colonial style

Around the Garrison

The layout of the Garrison lends itself to a circular tour, so start at the Main Guard and the cannon collection.

The **National Cannon Collection** is unique since it represents the largest assemblage of 17th-century English iron guns in the world and is one of only two collections that include a gun with Cromwell's Republican Arms. After Cromwell died orders were given for all his possessions to be destroyed, and the Barbados cannon with his crest is the only one to have been found on land – perhaps the order never reached the holder, who may have been in St Lucy. There are around 150 guns, about a dozen of which are posted in front of the Main Guard looking onto the Savannah, while others can be found at the museum in St Ann's Fort.

The **Main Guard**, built in 1804, is the centerpiece of the Garrison and houses two important features; the clock tower and the coat of arms. Courts martial and other matters were handled here, and a small guardhouse at the back of the building held prisoners. Today the Main Guard is home to the administrative headquarters of many military organizations, such as the Barbados Legion and the Poppy League.

The **clock tower** is dated 1803 and was made by Dwerri and Cater of London. The coat of arms on the front of the building also dates back to 1803. It was discovered by the former Garrison Secretary of the Regiment, Major Hartland, and is made of Coadestone, an artificial stone developed by Eleanor Coade around 1780. She died before revealing the formula for this durable clay substance, although efforts to discover the 'recipe' continue today. The coat of arms was painted white but the stone itself is actually tinged with pink. Another feature of this coat of arms is that the animals are couchant instead of in the rampant stance, which is more common.

The **Drill Hall** has a long history of different uses, beginning in 1790 as a soldiers' barracks. In 1822 it became an armory and from 1881 until the British left it served as the Garrison headquarters. After 1905 possession passed to the Barbados Government, who used it for a gymnasium and drill hall for the Volunteers Force (hence the name). Around this time it was rented out for public events, becoming one of the island's favored dance venues in the 1970s. Today it is the Defense Force officers' and sergeants' mess hall.

St Ann's Fort, also part of the Defense Force compound, has recently opened as a museum housing more pieces from the cannon collection. Its beveled stone walls form a hexagon enclosing 1½ acres (0.6ha). A look-out tower, built in the 1830s, served as part of the signal system and operated as a wireless station from 1914 to 1918, communicating with ships.

Above: at the races
Left: a man tunes in to the racing commentary

The **Naval Magazine**, extending under St Ann's Fort, is thought to have been built in the late 1700s. A tunnel leading out from it was probably used for the secret loading and unloading of arms.

East of the fort across Garrison Hill, **Brigade House** is now a clinic, but in 1819 it was the Brigade Major's quarters. After 1862 it became the chaplain's quarters. Nearby **Savannah Lodge**, now occupied by the Caribbean Conservation Association and the Museum Association of the Caribbean, was originally a store and was later converted into a private residence. In 1927, the government bought the property to house the Colonial Secretary and gave it its present name.

Letchworth, **Geneva** and **Rafeen** are now private homes, but were originally the Ordnance Hospital. It is thought that the main hospital building was Geneva. Built before the Great Hurricane of 1831, the hospital survived, mainly due to its extensive iron pillar supports, which also made it a good hurricane shelter. After 1855 it was converted into a recreation, library, and theater facility. The **Blocks 'A', 'B'** and **'C' Officers' Barracks** are now government offices. Blocks 'A' and 'B' were termed the 'New Barracks' in 1824, when they each housed 400 men. **Block 'C'** dates from 1807.

The Barbados Museum

The **Barbados Museum and Historical Society** (Mon–Sat 9am–5pm, Sun 2–6pm; tel: 427-0201) is a fascinating museum, housed in the former military prison that was built between 1817 and 1818. In 1933 the government leased the complex to the budding Barbados Museum and Historical Society, and it has remained here ever since. It is filled wall to wall with history, from its brickwork architecture to its many artifacts, ranging from Amerindian relics to modern art. The **Cunard Gallery** holds West Indian paintings and prints dating back to the 1600s, the **Jubilee Gallery** is the focus of the island's social and cultural development, and the **Temporary Exhibition Gallery** displays a wide range of visiting shows. The **library** contains a wealth of West Indian historical material, from plantation records to maps and genealogical records. Youngsters are catered for in the interactive **Children's Gallery**. The museum also organises a **Cultural Heritage Island Tour** two days a week.

Washington's Place

Bush Hill House is the oldest residence in the Garrison area, which existed from around 1719. It is where George Washington stayed when he visited Barbados for seven weeks in 1751. Now known as **George Washington House** (Mon–Sat 9am–4.30pm), the original two-story stone building was restored as part of a multimillion dollar project and opened as a museum in 2007.

The **watermill** and **bath house** near the complex entrance date from at least 1793, perhaps earlier. Outside the compound a

Right: precious museum exhibits

monument commemorates 'the 14 soldiers and one married woman' killed in the Barracks and Hospital during the Great Hurricane.

The Officers' Quarters for the Royal Artillery and Royal Engineers included **Horseshoe Manor**, **The Bungalow** and **Caledon**, formerly the Barbados Gallery of Art. The gallery, a small non-profit fine arts museum, is now closed and its works held in storage at the Barbados Museum until further funding can be obtained. The buildings have been too dramatically changed since their construction in 1824 to reveal much about their original design.

Stafford House was built in 1812 as a barracks for the Ordnance, or Royal Artillery, and later accommodated the military band and their instruments. The current facade masks the underlying brick and stone work.

The **Savannah**, now a racecourse, was originally a swamp which was used in dry periods for various purposes. By the early 19th century a link was discovered between yellow fever and mosquitoes, resulting in the installation of underground drainage trenches to keep the land perpetually free of water. The Savannah then became a year-round parade ground and sports arena.

3. Around Bridgetown *(see map, page 34)*

A half-day option linking the principal attractions around Bridgetown. It includes the Malibu Visitors Centre, the Mount Gay Rum Visitor Centre, Pelican Craft Centre, Medford Craft Village and the Tyrol Cot Heritage Village.

You may want to take advantage of the beach and lunch facilities at Malibu. If you do want to 'beach it' here, it's worth calling ahead. as they are occasionally fully booked by cruise ships.

Get onto the ABC Highway and drive to the Warrens roundabout. Continue on to University Hill. At the roundabout at the bottom of the hill take the

second exit to join Spring Garden Highway. Look for the Brighton exit – opposite the Workbench Factory – and turn right. When you come to the stop sign a few seconds later, turn right again and follow the road almost to its end. **Malibu Visitors Centre** (daily 9am–5pm with tours every half hour, except between 11am and noon; tel: 425-9393) is on the left.

Rum Can't Done

Of the many spirits tours Barbados has to offer, this is perhaps the most comprehensive; it combines a tour of the island's largest distillery and demonstrations of traditional barrel-making, with beach and watersports facilities. The center itself is unusually designed, with muted purples, greens, and blues in a mosaic of arches

Left: watching the Independence Day parade

and A-frame angles; the souvenir shop stocks specialty items, including products bearing the Malibu logo, attractive sea glass jewelry and other unusual local craft items.

The guided tour takes you into the distillery, where you can see the step-by-step fermenting, distilling, refining and aging process in action. Enthusiastic and well-informed guides reveal all kinds of fascinating information, including how by-products are used for everything from cures for arthritis to household cleansers. The tour continues to the barrel-making area where the coopers reconstruct white oak whisky barrels for rum aging and storage. The coopers also make novelty items and furniture from the spent barrels.

The tour price includes access to the beachside center, where you can stay all day if you like. You are free to make use of the center's lovely beach and lounge chairs, changing rooms, showers, and lockers. There is also a bar and huge barbecue for lunches (11.30am–2.30pm), along with a watersports concession where you can rent gear. The center offers a variety of packages including a pass for visitors who want to spend the day.

If you also want to take in Mount Gay on your tour, go back to Spring Garden Highway. Since there is no right turn, you have to travel back to the Da Costa Mannings sign (at the Ham Center) and turn around. Drive the length of the highway towards town and look for the Mount Gay sign and a left turn signposted Exmouth.

Mount Gay (Mon–Fri 9.30am–3.30pm, Sat morning only; tours every 45 minutes; tel: 425-9066) is one of the world's oldest distilleries. The 30-minute tour includes a video presentation and a tour of the distillery, bottling plant, and aging area. This is another informative tour rich in detailed history spanning three centuries. In fact, there is evidence of rum-making dating as far back as 1703 on the Mount Gay estate in St Lucy, the island's northernmost parish. While all the guides are knowledgeable and amiable, perhaps the best-known is head barman Christopher, who provides an animated sampling experience at the end of the tour.

On leaving Mount Gay turn left on to the Highway and take a right at the traffic lights if you would like to join or find out more about one of the exciting tours on the **Atlantis Submarine** (tours Tues–Sat; tel: 436-8929). Atlantis Submarines offer guests three ways to experience Barbados' underwater world: the submarine and Seatrec (semi-submersible) tours are both 1½ hours long;

Above: golden girl
Right: bottling liquid gold at Mount Gay

the capital & environs

snorkel tours run to at least 2 hours. To reach the Atlantis office continue to the roundabout and take the right-hand exit to the Shallow Draught. Veer to the compound on your right, and there you will see the imposing multi-decked **MV *Harbour Master*** (tel: 430-0900) at dock, loosely styled on a Mississippi steamboat. Harbour Master offer day and evening cruise packages on the 600-passenger, four-deck vessel. Guests can enjoy dinner, dancing, and live entertainment on board.

Also docked at Shallow Draught is the ***Jolly Roger*** pirate ship that has a selection of fun party cruises, where the music is very loud and there is plenty of rum punch to go around.

Arts and Crafts

Take a slight detour south of the harbour area to the outskirts of Bridgetown, to the **Pelican Craft Centre**. Leave the harbour complex and continue straight on at the roundabout in to Harbour Road. The craft center will come into view at the end of this road. At the junction turn left on to Princess Alice Highway where there is parking immediately on your left.

Allow a little time to wander around this collection of small shops specializing in locally-made, handcrafted souvenirs. Many of the items on sale are of good quality, such as alluring batik cloth skillfully made into attractive clothing and home accessories. There are wonderful creative works made from all manner of materials including ceramic, wood, shells, and glass, and delightful art exhibits that feature both sculptures and paintings. The centre is at its busiest when there is a cruise ship docked at the nearby port, and the passengers head to the Pelican to explore the shops.

Almost next door to the craft center is the **Caribbean Cigar Company** (tel: 437-8519), where visitors can take a free tour around the factory to see how the cigars are made. The company specializes in two lines of premium handmade smokes made from Cuban tobacco.

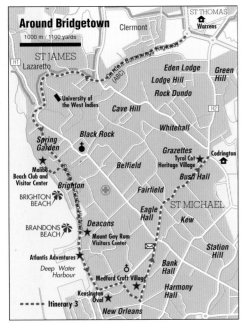

Next stop is **Medford Craft Village** (Mon–Fri 8am–5pm, Sat 8.30am–1pm), the island's hub of Mahogany crafts. To get to Medford from the Pelican Craft Centre return the way you came and head towards Spring Garden Highway, but this time go straight on at the traffic lights. In less than a mile you will see the small yellow sign (on the left) directing visitors to Medford Craft Village. Turn right, and at the stop sign turn left into Baxter's Road; just a few yards ahead is Medford's yellow wall and entrance.

This is a real behind-the-scenes look at mahogany craft production.

You can watch the skilful artisans at work and browse for souvenirs, gifts and art treasures. The real treat is the main Medford shop, selling work of a quality rarely seen in the retail outlets around the island, including magnificent, highly polished coffee tables and ornately carved chairs, as well as beautiful abstract 'root art' made from the roots of mahogany trees, and Medford's well-known mahogany clock collection.

A Stately Home

Coming out of Medford Craft Village turn left on the highway to the **Tyrol Cot Heritage Village** (weekdays 9am–5pm) and through the bustling little suburb of Eagle Hall. Go straight on at the traffic lights and follow the road to Codrington Hill. Tyrol Cot is on the left before the traffic lights.

One of the Barbados National Trust's heritage sites, Tyrol Cot was the home of the late Sir Grantley Adams, Barbados' first premier, and his wife Lady Adams from 1929 until her death in 1990, and it was here that they raised their one son, J. M. G. M 'Tom' Adams, the island's second prime minister. The house was a hive of political activity from the 1930s to the 1960s, when Sir Grantley was fighting for the rights of the working class.

The house was built in 1854 by William Farnum, a prominent local builder. It is an excellent example of 19th-century sturdy architecture, with its blend of modest Palladian, classical, and tropical vernacular elements. The interior has high ceilings, arched doorways, classical jalousied windows, and antique furniture owned by the Adams family, including a Victorian revolving bookcase, a Regency-style double-ended couch, and many handcrafted Barbadian mahogany pieces. The house is filled with the Adams' personal memorabilia.

On the 3 acres (1.2ha) of landscaped grounds the National Trust has developed a craft village using the chattel house blueprint for the shops and studios that house the artists and their work, including silk-screening, leathercraft, and basketry outlets. Here too are replica slave quarters, a working blacksmith's, a rum shop and the Sweetie Shop.

To head home from Tyrol Cot, continue up the hill to the ABC Highway.

Above: Tyrol Cot, the childhood home of Tom Adams

The Platinum Coast

4. HOLETOWN, ST JAMES, AND BEYOND *(see map, p38)*

A leisurely trip up the island's west coast includes visits to St James Parish Church, Folkestone Marine Park, Mullins Beach, and the Sir Frank Hutson Sugar Museum and Portvale Sugar Factory. With stops for swimming and shopping, you can make a whole day of this tour.

This is an easy drive in terms of directions as you stay on the same road for most of the trip, driving up Highway 1 to Speightstown. If you are staying on the west coast, you can join Highway 1 at whatever point is convenient.

From the south coast take the ABC Highway to the Warrens roundabout, continuing straight over to University Hill. As you descend the hill there is a lovely view of the harbor straight ahead. The clusters of white buildings you pass on the way are part of the University of the West Indies (UWI), which was established in 1948 and reached full university status in 1962.

At the roundabout at the bottom of the hill, turn right and drive up the west coast.

Along the 5-mile (8-km) drive to Holetown are a number of windows to the sea. Tourist activity increases as you continue north, reaching a bustling level at the bottom of Holders Hill, where there are a number of quaint boutiques and antiques shops. Along the way is **Blue Monkey**, a delightful beach bar with an attractive vista of Paynes Bay.

North of Holders Hill trees line the approach road to **Sandy Lane Hotel**. This elegant hotel rose to prominence in the 1960s and 70s when it attracted a star-studded guest list. In 1998, in a controversial redevelopment, the old coral-stone building was demolished. Today, the hotel looks surprisingly similar to the original, complete with sweeping staircase and dance floor. Facilities include high tech room amenities, a spa, and a championship golf course designed by Tom Fazio. To swim here or walk along the shore, take the public beach entrance at the south end of the hotel; alternatively you can walk up from Paynes Bay.

Historic Holetown

As you enter **Holetown** proper, you will notice the brightly painted **Chattel House Village** on the right. Opened in late 1996, the village is a cluster of chattel house-style shops fashioned after its sister St Lawrence Gap village in Christ Church. A browse through the village is an enjoyable shopping

Above: a Paynes Bay vista

platinum coast

experience (the entrance is at the Sandy Crest Medical Centre turn-off opposite the Chefette fast food outlet).

There are two major shopping malls in Holetown: **Sunset Crest Plazas** 1 and 2, which have a lively mix, including a supermarket, duty-free outlets, local shops, and eating places. On the other side of the road is a selection of beach-side restaurants. Try **Cocomos**, which has an appealing Caribbean ambiance and where you can have a drink at the water's edge, or the **Surfside** restaurant, tucked away behind the Parish Post Office and Police Station. If you prefer a light snack instead try **Patisserie Flindt** for its sumptuous pastries. In front of the Police Station, the **Holetown Monument** commemorates the 1625 landing of the first English settlers. Erected in 1905, this monument bears the wrong date of the landing, an error that was eventually corrected with another plaque in 1975.

Out of Town

Coming out of Holetown on the left is **St James Church**, site of the island's first church. The original wooden church was replaced by a stone building in the late 1600s, but was destroyed in the 1780 hurricane; most of the present church dates from the 1800s; in the 1980s the building was restored to its present state. It contains many historic artifacts, including the baptismal font from 1684 and the original church bell, which pre-dates the United States' Liberty Bell by more than 50 years.

Traveling for 1 mile (1.6km) north of Holetown, you will come to the government-run **Folkestone Marine Park and Visitor Center** (park open daily; shops Mon–Fri 9am–5pm). Folkestone has a good beach, many water-based facilities and activities, freshwater showers, and shops, as well as a small and fairly basic interpretive center and museum with marine and coastal environment displays, exhibits of the island's fishing industry and a marine aquarium.

The underwater park zone extends offshore from Sandy Lane north to Colony Club; here you can rent gear for snorkeling around the fringe reef, hire a boat for diving, or take a trip in a glass-bottom boat that plies the area. Divers can also explore the wreck of the *Stavronikita*, which lies in 120ft (37m) of water less than half a mile from shore. The park, like other favored dive and snorkel

Above: an old Barbadian man
Right: palm-protected Paynes Bay Hotel

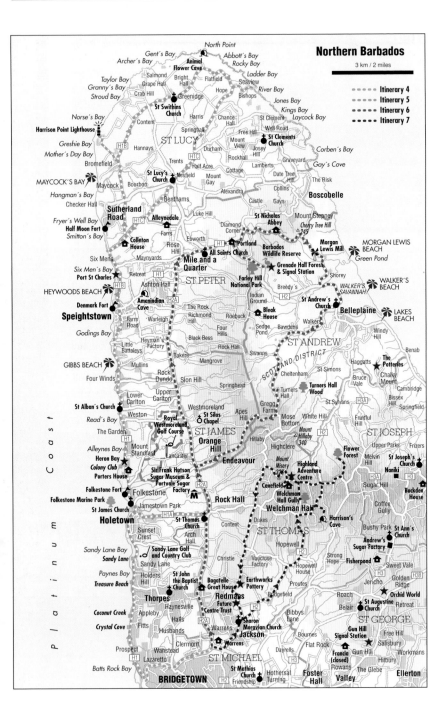

Northern Barbados

3 km / 2 miles

- - - - Itinerary 4
- - - - Itinerary 5
- - - - Itinerary 6
- - - - Itinerary 7

spots on the island, reveals a rich underwater world of living coral, small colorful fish, sea anemone, and occasionally larger fish such as barracuda.

Northern Shores

Less than 1 mile (1.6km) north of Folkestone you will come to the **Colony Club** beach entrance. In addition to being a lovely beach, this spot offers a peek at **Heron Bay House**, built in 1947 by the late Ronald Tree, a member of Winston Churchill's British parliament. This house, where he often wintered, enjoyed a steady stream of movie stars, heads of state, and royalty, including Princess Margaret, Sir Winston and Lady Churchill, Sophia Loren, Ingrid Bergman, Pierre Trudeau, and Adlai Stevenson. Designed by English architect Sir Geoffrey Jellico, Heron Bay is a Palladian villa based on the Villa Maser design. Set in 20 acres (8ha) of magnificently landscaped grounds with huge gardens and wooded areas, the main coral stone wings form a semicircle around the courtyard, where a massive chandelier hangs. The complex includes a number of other buildings, such as the pink house, with its octagonal windows. The National Trust Open Houses Program (every Wednesday from January to April) sometimes includes this property on its list.

We now travel past a stretch of opulent properties and homes that line the beach along the coast to Speightstown. This scenic drive wends northwards and soon opens out onto magnificent **Mullins Beach**. This is a perfect spot to enjoy the sun and take a dip, if you are in the mood. There are motorized watersports here too, such as waterskiing and jet skis. Visitors can take a boat excursion to a spot offshore of Mount Standfast, to see large sea turtles. If you wish to feed the creatures, bags of fish

Above: all the diving equipment you need
Right: relaxing at Mannie's Suga Suga beach bar

can be purchased from stalls on the shore near the turtle site. Mullins also has an elegant beachside restaurant and bar with shower facilities.

Head back south towards Holetown, but before you actually get to the town, take the left hand turn onto Highway 1A that leads inland, just after the bridge. Take this road to the roundabout and drive north on Highway 2A for less than 1 mile (1.6km) to reach the **Sir Frank Hutson Sugar Museum** and **Portvale Sugar Factory** (Mon–Sat 9am–5pm). Managed by the National Trust, the museum, in the old boiling house, is small but packed with interesting artifacts, equipment, and photos depicting scenes from the early days of the sugar industry. Between January and May you can tour the working Portvale Factory and watch sugar manufacturing in action, from its genesis as cane to its crystalline conclusion. You can also learn about the rigorous production controls, and the steps to make such by-products as 'cane syrup' and molasses.

You can take one of two routes back to your base from here. Go back the way you came if you want to shop in Holetown or make a beach stop. To head directly home, stay on Highway 2A to the Warrens roundabout, and then back to the ABC Highway.

5. FROM SPEIGHTSTOWN TO ST LUCY *(see map, p38)*

This is a day tour of the spectacular north coast, which begins in Speightstown and includes Harrison Point lighthouse, Animal Flower Cave, North Point, and River Bay. It is recommended that you take a picnic, grab a bite at Pirate's Tavern, or dine in a Speightstown eatery.

St Lucy is often overlooked by visitors because it lacks the developed attractions of other parishes, but if you enjoy exploring areas slightly off the beaten track, this tour makes an excellent day out. Follow the west coast itinerary and continue on past Mullins Beach until you reach Speightstown.

The narrow streets, two-story balconied buildings and the little fishing boats that dot the beaches combine to make Speightstown special. For over 300 years the town has been a primary seaport of Barbados, it is one of the last

18th-century ports in the Caribbean region. In the mid-1600s the area was fiercely loyal to Charles I and its shores were lined with small forts that repelled Oliver Cromwell's ships. Popularly known as 'Little Bristol' for its trading links with Bristol in England, it was named Speightstown after William Speight, the owner of the land where the town stands.

Today Speightstown is the main shopping center in the north, although its architecture is somewhat faded and decaying. There are plans to restore and preserve the town's heritage, and to renew economic activity.

The **Gallery of Caribbean Art** is in the Northern Business Centre on the main throughfare. Here you'll find paintings and sculptures by well-known, accomplished artists from all over the the Caribbean region.

If you are hungry try **Mango's By the Sea** which is run by a friendly Canadian couple and offers good service and reasonable prices. For more local color, try the **Fisherman's Pub**, a bustling beachside eatery and bar specializing in authentic Bajan-style foods, accompanied by the pulsating beat of calypso.

Driving north, away from Speightstown, you will pass the exclusive Port St Charles residential complex on the left. Here a number of luxurious condominiums have been built around a marina. These are homes for the well-heeled, and some celebrities have second homes here too.

A little further along, travel through **Six Men's Bay**, a busy little fishing area with colorful boats lining the beachfront. Friday night is fish fry in the village – more low key than the fish fry at Oistins, but fun just the same because the fish is fresh and the local rum flows. The road soon cuts inland, linking up to Highway 1B going north. At this point the route runs through flat drab land and housing developments, but once you reach the coast, you will be sure to agree that it was well worth the drive.

North Point

A sign indicates a left turn for **Harrison Point Lighthouse**, one of three lighthouses still in operation on the island. Following this road, which narrows as you get closer to the lighthouse, you pass the Barbados Youth Service headquarters, formerly a United States Naval base. From here the road turns into what is locally called a 'cart road' – a narrow dirt track – but it's safe to drive through. Today, the working lighthouses are maintained but unmanned. From the cliff you can see the start of the rugged north coast.

Come out from the lighthouse and continue north to your next stop, which is well signposted. The **Animal Flower Cave** (daily 9am–4pm) was a little

Left: a window to the ocean in the Animal Flower Cave
Top: Speightstown's fading architecture

neglected at one point, but it has been revived and now enjoys a steady stream of visitors. It was named after the tiny sea anemones (sea worms) that once lived in the rock pools.

Close to North Point, the northernmost part of Barbados, this is the island's only accessible sea cave, discovered in 1780 by two English explorers. Its coral floor is estimated to be 400,000 to 500,000 years old and the 'younger' coral section above the floor about 126,000 years old. The dating was carried out by the German Geographical Institute, and visitors can see a 'map' of the dating work in the bar-restaurant. The cave now stands some 6ft (1.8m) above the high tide mark, even though it was formed at sea level. This is because Barbados is rising by about 1inch (2.5cm) per 1,000 years.

The management of the cave also runs the bar-restaurant **Pirate's Tavern**, and has a well-trained and amiable group of guides to take small groups of visitors into the cave for a nominal fee. The first thing to notice is the huge coral stairway leading down into the cave. Built around 1912, these steps are a remnant from the cave's days as a dancehall, when people from around the island arrived at the north coast by horse and buggy for a weekend of seaside relaxation, entertainment, and fun.

Down in the cave guides will point out formations and any of the now rare sea anemones, locally called 'animal flowers,' as well as other artifacts from bygone days, including the braces in the coral ceiling where lanterns once hung. The view out of the huge limestone caverns to the sea is breathtaking. The land around the entrance to the cave consists of barren rock, much like a moonscape; it's difficult to imagine that sugar cane was grown here in the 18th century. On calm days you can also go into a 'room' off to the right and swim in the natural pool, or at least take in yet another awesome view of the Atlantic through this larger sea window. When conditions get too rough, access to the cave closes.

Back up on dry land, the bar-restaurant serves refreshing drinks and hearty sandwiches. Its walls and ceiling are covered in business cards from around the world, and the staff will happily loan you the glue to add your own. This substantial collection has been amassing since the early 1970s when the cave first opened to the public.

Outside the bar area are a few cannons recovered from ships that did not survive the vigorous waves of the Atlantic. At one time they included one of the few known cannons to bear the crest of Oliver Cromwell (this particular cannon is now on display in Main Guard, forming part of the Garrison's National Cannon Collection, *see page 30*).

Above: scene from the north

You can continue a little further to the **Benab Café** which has crafts for sale, made by Guyanese Amerindians. Benab means meeting house in Amerindian and owner and cook Guyanese-born James Barrow, a local copperwork artist, is dedicated to preserving Amerindian culture. He is a fount of knowledge and loves to share his experiences with interested visitors.

Coastal Views

The sea's fury has carved a magnificent cove at **North Point**, not far from the Animal Flower Cave, so even if the cave is closed due to angry seas it's well worth going there for the rugged coastal views. This is one of the island's pristine panoramas. The sea's rhythmic drubbing of the landscape has a mesmerizing effect that, for all its roar, is tranquilizing. On windy days the salty spray splashes over the rocks in huge arches.

From here the craggy coastline continues eastwards to **River Bay**. A freshwater river runs down to the sea. At the junction, turn left and descend to the car park, picnicking areas, and amenities. While swimming in the mouth of the river and the sea beyond is discouraged (currents are very strong), a little wade in the shallow 'river' inlet is harmless. Popular with locals, this is an ideal picnic spot with lovely shaded areas and picnic tables all along both sides of the river. Both children and adults will enjoy climbing around and exploring the area, Although it is often busy at weekends the bay is usually pretty quiet during the week. There are staffed bathroom facilities and a freshwater shower.

From here make your way back, cutting inland to pass through the rural north (you will see a left-hand turn soon after leaving River Bay: follow that all the way to the roundabout, on Highway 1C and Duncan O'Neal Highway, and return along Highway 2A, the road above the Highway 1 coast road). Alternatively, return the way you came, stopping for a little shopping en route.

Top: the rugged coast at North Point

The Northeast Scenic Region

6. NORTHERN HIGHLIGHTS *(see map, p38)*

This is a full day of interesting sights, including the Wildlife Reserve and Grenade Hall Signal Station, Farley Hill Park, and a tour of the 17th-century plantation house, St Nicholas Abbey. Visit Cherry Tree Hill for fabulous views and see Morgan Lewis Mill, the Caribbean region's last intact sugar windmill.

If your hotel packs picnic lunches, or if you have facilities to prepare one yourself, take a picnic on this tour, as Farley Hill is perfect for a relaxing lunch. If not, you can drive down to Speightstown between stops.

This is a long itinerary so start out early. Get on the ABC Highway and exit at the Warrens roundabout and go north onto Highway 2A. Travel up to Mile And A Quarter junction in St Peter. Turn right, travel about half a mile (0.8km) and then right onto the Charles Duncan O'Neal Highway.

Monkey Business

Follow the signs to the **Barbados Wildlife Reserve** and **Grenade Hall Signal Station** (daily 10am– 5pm). The admission fee covers both attractions. The 4-acre (1.6ha) Wildlife Reserve, opened in 1985, was initially a woodland sanctuary for the indigenous Barbados green monkey and a few other local and regional creatures, such as tortoise, the tiny Brocket deer, and birds, including brown pelicans and peacocks. Over the years stock has increased and the reserve is now home to an intriguing menagerie. Take your time going through the meandering mahogany lined paths, and move along quietly. If you breeze through too quickly or make too much noise you may miss seeing some of the more shy creatures.

The reserve has several animals native to the region, including the agouti (a red-eared guinea pig-like creature), hares, which were once common in Barbados, the alligator-like Caiman from Guyana, porcupine, and iguana. You may also see pink flamingos, maras (from Africa), wallaby, otters, and snakes, and the reserve has an aviary of mostly macaws and cockatoos.

What makes this stop so much fun is that most of the area is open, so animals run about freely. You may be hard-pressed to see monkeys as they tend to roam to other areas; however, try a visit around feeding time (3pm) and you'll be sure to see them.

The snack bar and reception area of the reserve are beautifully finished

Above: woodland sanctuary has ancient trees

in a rustic design using sugar factory relics. The bricks forming the pathways are also made from old sugar factory buildings.

Just next door – on the same compound – is Grenade Hall Signal Station and forest area. A visit to the restored signal station gives an insight into how the military communicated in the 19th century. Six of these stations were constructed at vantage points around the island, and by using semaphore the military could send messages island-wide in a matter of minutes. The station has a display of artifacts, both military and pre-Columbian, and an audio loop recounts the drama of the 1816 slave revolt and other episodes in the island's history when this communication network was used.

Behind the signal station a 3-mile (5-km) rambling coral pathway takes you through a thriving woodland. Amusing 'question & answer' signs posted along the way bring this ecosystem to life and provide information about tropical forests, folk medicine, and conservation.

Parks and Plantations

Across the road is **Farley Hill National Park** (daily 7am–6pm; admission fee per car), an idyllic spot for a picnic lunch with a stunning panorama. This was the site of the magnificent 19th-century 'great house' Farley Hill, considered the island's most stately mansion. In 1956 the house was the

location for several scenes in the movie, *Island in the Sun*, which starred Harry Belafonte, but soon after it was destroyed by fire. Its ruins make for an interesting backdrop to the 17 acres (7ha) of land. The government bought the property in 1965 and the following year Queen Elizabeth II officially opened Farley Hill as a park.

If you are not picnicking, return to Mile And A Quarter and head back

Above: Grenade Hall Signal Station
Left: ruins of Farley Hill

into Speightstown for lunch. As on the Platinum Coast tour, **Fisherman's Pub** is a good option with relatively low prices, plenty of daily specials to choose from and a welcoming ambience.

Jacobean Abbey

Either return to Mile And A Quarter, or if you are coming from Farley Hill, go back to the start of the Charles Duncan O'Neal Highway and turn right onto Highway 1. From here follow signposts to **St Nicholas Abbey** (Sun–Fri 10am–3.30pm); the drive from Farley Hill is no more than 10–15 minutes. The Great House has been restored and work on the surrounding estate buildings is continuing. There are plans to put the steam mill that grinds the sugar cane back into action and manufacture the St Nicholas brand of sugar, rum and molasses.

Built between 1650 and 1660, St Nicholas Abbey is one of the few remaining Jacobean homes in the western hemisphere. The house is magnificently furnished much as it was 300 years ago. While many furnishings have come and gone with its various owners, several pieces date back to the 17th and 18th centuries. Of special note is the grandfather clock, which stands on the staircase. Made by J Thwaites of London in 1759, it has occupied the same spot for more than 200 years. A tour of the property includes most of the downstairs, the 'backyard' with its 'four-seater' outhouse, and the original bath house equipped with tubs and an old-fashioned water heating apparatus.

The early history of St Nicholas Abbey's ownership is as colorful as the furnishings. Its original owner was Benjamin Beringer, but after scandals involving land squabbles, sexual affairs, and a murder, John Yeamans emerged as the property's second owner. He was knighted, and soon after was appointed Governor of South Carolina, a post he took up in 1672.

The property passed through many hands, usually by inheritance, but in the early 1800s it was bought out of Chancery Court (debt). Lieutenant Colonel Stephen Cave, one of a long line of Caves who have owned the property since then, inherited the abbey in 1964, and lived there part-time until his death in 2003.

St Nicholas Abbey's 420 acres (170ha) of plantation land extends to **Cherry Tree Hill** (turn left as you leave the abbey). The road there leads

through heavy canopies of trees then opens out to a lovely panorama of the East coast. Continuing down this road brings you to **Morgan Lewis Mill** (daily 9am–5pm), used for grinding cane in the 18th and 19th centuries. The only intact sugar windmill in the Caribbean, it is on the World Monuments Fund list of 100 Most Endangered Sites in the World. The Dutch influenced mill is a typical example of the island's two centuries long tradition of wind-powered cane grinding. It has undergone major restoration work and you can still see the fully intact wheel house and sails.

Left: Morgan Lewis sugar mill

Driving back to your base, you can take one of two routes – either continue south a mile or so (about 1.6km) until you meet the Charles Duncan O'Neal Highway and take that back past Farley Hill and the Reserve to return the way you came, or if you want to see another side of Barbados, continue past the highway and travel through the maze of scenic but confusing roads that cut through the Scotland District to Highway 2A. Armed with your map, a sense of direction, humor, and patience, you can amble through sleepy villages and pick your way back. Views on the way are magnificent, and you will see the real heart of the island.

At least three routes will lead you to Highway 2A. The best of these is Orange Hill via Gregg Farm. However, if you miss that one, there are other routes which also connect to 2A. Signs may help, but don't depend on them as many are in disrepair and unreadable. The most important thing is to roll with it and head west to Highway 2A.

7. THE GARDEN HEARTLAND *(see map, p38)*

This is a full-day tour through the heart of Barbados with visits to three of the island's biggest attractions: Harrison's Cave, Flower Forest, and Welchman Hall Gully. On the return, it makes a shopping stop at Earthworks and The Potters House.

Harrison's Cave has some very busy periods when passengers from the cruise ships visit, so it is worth calling well in advance to make a booking (tel: 438-6640); otherwise you may have to wait in line for a long time.

Make your way on to the ABC Highway and exit at the Jackson roundabout. After driving through the little village of Jackson, you will see the old **Sharon Moravian Church** on your left. The Moravians, who came to Barbados in 1765, were the first missionaries to educate the slaves and introduce them to Christianity. Sharon, built in 1799, was seriously damaged in the Great Hurricane of 1831, but rebuilt in 1834.

Continue on this road for a few miles and follow signs to **Harrison's Cave** (daily, first tour 9am, last tour 4pm). Filled with streams, cascading water, pools, and stalactites and stalagmites, this is one of the finest natural caverns in the region. While historical records of the cave date back to 1796, it remained unexplored until 1970. After considerable development, the cave was opened to the public in 1981 and has become one of the island's top attractions. Tours are conducted by trams, which travel down into the cave every half hour. A slide presentation is shown before the tour and there is a short but colorful nature walk around the property, which you can take

Above: walking home past the cane fields

before or after the tour, plus a Visitor Center, refreshment stand, and hand-icraft shop. About 1 mile (1.6km) from the cave is **Springvale Eco Heritage Museum and Tours** (Mon–Sat 10am–4pm; Sun by appointment only), an interactive museum with characters such as a mauby seller, basket weaver, and a washer woman, complete with wash pan and jukking board. There are also nature trails along which visitors can discover traditional crops, and plants with medicinal properties.

A Walk in the Woods

Next on this itinerary is the Flower Forest. Leaving Harrison's Cave, continue north (right) to the Bloomsbury junction with the little 'bamboo village' (industrious locals have converted this area into a bustling handicraft center that is popular with cruise ship passengers and other island tours). Turn right; just ahead the bridge wall on your left offers a stunning view of the eastern coast. You may want to stop and examine the wares of local hawkers.

Continue on this twisting road, passing a large dairy farm. You will see signs indicating when to turn left for the **Flower Forest** (daily 9am–5pm). Described as a cross between a botanical garden and a nature trail, this is a 50-acre (20ha) explosion of greenery with commanding vistas of the Scotland District. You can take from an hour to a day to stroll along the paths and see a won-derland of tropical plants, from gorgeous blooms to magnificent trees. Time for a light lunch and browse in the gift shop in the main lobby.

After the Flower Forest, make your way back to the 'bamboo village,' this time turning right to carry on to Welchman Hall Gully, which is around the corner from Harrison's Cave. Owned and operated by the Barbados National Trust, **Welchman Hall Gully** (daily 9am–5pm) is about a 1-mile (1.6-km) hike through a deep, densely wooded gully filled with a variety of trees, plants, and flowers. It formed part of the network of caves linked to Harri-son's until its roof collapsed to form a gully, and this is why it is so much

Above: Harrison's Cave

deeper than the hundreds of other gullies that ribbon the island. It has been tended since 1860 when the then owners introduced a variety of exotic plants and blooms to its already rich vegetation. Later, the gully fell into neglect until it was adopted by the Trust in 1962, becoming the first organized natural site in Barbados.

Today the gully is rich in every shade of green imaginable. You will encounter large, impressive stands of bamboo, splashes of colorful flowers, and massive decorative and fruit-bearing trees. As you reach the end of the trail, the scent of nutmeg may waft past, and on the ground you may see the web-like pieces of mace that cover the nutmeg. The trail is well-marked and, with the brochure to guide you, it is easy to identify the trees and blooms. The silence is broken only occasionally by squawking birds or monkeys crashing around in the trees above.

Leaving Welchman Hall, turn left for the brief drive to **Highland Adventure Centre** (tel: 431-8928), where you can stop for refreshments, enjoy the stunning view. The Adventure Centre is perched between the island's highest points and offers a real adventure through 1,500 acres (610ha) of previously inaccessible land, much of it privately owned. Guides lead excursions through four parishes, delivering one exciting panorama after another. The tours vary in length – from two hours to a whole day – and mode. You can walk (only in a group of 20 or more) or travel by mountain bike (mostly downhill). The day-long tour is a 5-mile (8-km) hike to the east coast.

The Potteries

An adventurous route home through the heartland area also takes in additional attractions. Turn right out of Highland Adventure Centre and about a mile (1.6km) ahead is the Challenor School for the mentally handicapped on your left. Here take a right turn to go around the second highest point on the island, **Mount Misery**. This meandering road will ultimately lead you on to Highway D, a well-paved, wide road. Turn left and follow the road past the old Vaucluse factory and on to Shop Hill, following signs for a left-hand turn to **Earthworks Pottery** (Mon–Fri 9am–5pm, Sat 9am–1pm). Master potter Goldie Spieler has carved a special niche for herself in this eyrie. You can buy beautiful functional art works from her studio, which is operated by her son David. The Spielers are famous for their hand-finished and decorated tableware with a distinctive Caribbean flavor. In the **Potter's House**, artist

Vanita Comissiong runs **On The Wall Gallery**, with another branch at Champers Restaurant *(see page 73)*, where she sells bold, brightly colored paintings by a selection of Caribbean artists. Also on the site is a batik studio and an excellent small café with a great view.

Heading home, go down the hill to the junction by the Sharon Moravian Church. Turn right here to go back to the Jackson roundabout and home.

Left: a potter at work

The East

8. THE ATLANTIC COAST *(see map, p52)*

A full day exploring the east coast. Drive up the East Coast Road and into Scotland District's picturesque Chalky Mount and the potteries. Visit a batik gallery, go down to the famous 'soup bowl' and Bathsheba, and lunch at the Atlantis Hotel with its fabulous overlook. Afterwards visit Andromeda Botanic Gardens.

If you do this tour on a Sunday, it is worth knowing that the Atlantis has a popular buffet lunch.

To reach the east coast, take the ABC highway to the Lower Estate exit. This is not a roundabout, but a turn-off located between the Hothersal and Norman Niles roundabouts. Drive the few miles to the stop sign, then turn right onto what is Highway 3, though no signs tell you that.

The 30-minute drive to the east is both scenic and varied. Along the way you will see wavy lines of chattel houses among the cane fields and pass through backwater villages where time seems to stand still. Half way along, just after **Market Hill** village, with its gas station and few stores, you will come to a three-way junction where a sign, half-buried under the canes, directs you left to the east coast. Soon after this you will pass **Andrew's Sugar Factory**, one of only two sugar factories remaining in Barbados, the other is Portvale *(see page 40)* in St James. Depending on the time of year, you may see the great steam generators in action, breathing life into the cane grinding process. If it is cane grinding time (February to May), drive with extra care because the cane trucks on the road are large, cumbersome, and very slow.

At Parris Hill the road curves right and the coral walls are covered in community art. Continue on, passing the Grantley Adams School and the police station. From here it is literally all down hill. As you descend Horse Hill you will get your first view of the rugged east coast, and the 10–15-minute descent is punctuated with glimpses of what's to come. Turn left at the sign for **Naniki Restaurant**, which serves Caribbean cuisine. Drive carefully as the road is narrow, steep in sections, and full of twists and turns, leading to a stunning panorama of lush hillsides with colorful anthuriums.

Eventually you will come to a junction. The roads here, in any direction, are worth exploring. However, we will go left and start our tour with a drive

Above: on a Sunday morning hike in the Scotland district

the east

down to the East Coast Road. The steep road winds past groves of banana trees to meet the Atlantic coast. Here, you will find a stark contrast to the tranquil waters of the west and south. This area known as **Cattlewash**, has a relentless breeze and a heavy surf pounds the beach, peppering it with traces of tar, flotsam from passing ships, and driftwood. Explore the exposed reef and rock pools at low tide (swimming is very dangerous here), but keep an eye out for jellyfish. Along the coast are weathered beach houses, popular local holiday spots.

The hills to the left are the Scotland District, supposedly reminiscent of the Scottish Highlands. Nestling among them is a heavily wooded area, **Barclays Park** – a good picnic area. Drive on to the Belleplaine junction.

Clay and Crafts

At the Belleplaine Potteries shop take a sharp left and follow the road past the petrol station and the Government Agricultural Station. About half a mile (0.8km) further on a sign points left to Chalky Mount. Turn here, passing the Chalky Mount School, and make your way up Coggins Hill. At the crest, a sign directs you left to the Potteries. (You will also see a sign directing you right: this is to a private potter's residence, which you can visit on your way out.) The Potteries is less than half a mile (0.8km) further on, but before stopping there follow the road to the end for a short hike to the top of Chalky Mount for the view. (Park out of the way as buses use this open area to turn around.) Chalky Mount juts up from the coast to about 550ft (168m) above sea level and offers one of the finest views on the island.

Coming back out, stop off at the **Potteries** (Mon–Fri 8am–5pm; Sat–Sun 8am–3pm). While

Top: play time in Belleplaine
Right: at the Potteries

this entire village was once bustling with potters working from their homes, only two potters work like this today. Yet the art is not dead, it has simply been centralized and most of the potters now work in one place. The potters here will gladly show you how they work, and may even demonstrate the old manual 'kick wheel' on display, a 300-year-old pot-shaping method used until recently.

There is a nice range of work for sale, many pieces in muted tones. You can find decorative items as well as traditional pottery, such as 'monkey pots' and coal pots, which are both functional and good souvenirs. There is a wide selection of vases, plates, mugs, pitchers, candle shades, and other items, including miniature pottery chattel houses.

On the way back from the Potteries, just before turning back onto East Coast Road, stop off at **Belleplaine Pottery** (daily), an interesting co-op shop. The owner has a small bar and sells work by potters in the area. He also has a little garden with animals in the back.

Afterwards, return along the East Coast Road climbing to Cleavers Hill and you will see the batik signs directing you to **John C Mayers Batik Gallery**. John works from his home and during the week he is there most of the time. The artist's colorful, folklore themed batiks have been exhibited locally and overseas.

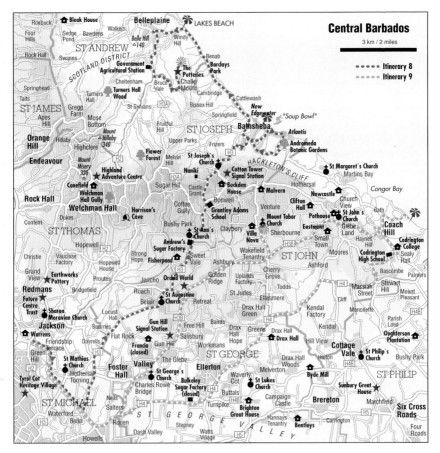

Surf and Turf

Continue down the hill and just before the bottom turn left along a small road. Follow this for just a few minutes to enter the famous 'soup bowl' area, popular with surfers. There is a small parking area, and you can take a stroll if you like.

A little further along the road are two pleasing refreshment stops: **Round House Inn**, which was originally an elegant 19th-century home, has good food with a dash of local flair (it can be busy at lunchtimes); and the **New Edgewater**, with its 'olde-worlde' charm – both have breathtaking views of the rocky coastline.

Travel back past the soup bowl using the same route but this time veer left into **Bathsheba**. You will pass the popular **Bonito Bar** whose upstairs seating offers a good view of the surfing action. From here make your way up the hill (park at the bottom and walk if you feel like it), passing the Community Center with its mural depicting famous Barbadians.

Just past the Center is a left turn for the **Atlantis Hotel**, one of the best lunch stops on the coast (daily 11.30am–3pm). Perching on a ledge above the sea, the Atlantis is over 100 years old, its popularity is a tribute to the legendary hotelier, Enid Maxwell, who ran the place for over 50 years. Secure a table on its balcony and watch the waves and the fishing activity while you eat. On Sundays, the hotel serves a buffet lunch, a fabulous spread of Bajan foods, for about US$25, there is another buffet lunch special on Wednesday; and the rest of the week it offers an excellent full Bajan 'plate' lunch, with a choice of fish or chicken, for around US$20.

Coming out of the Atlantis, continue up the hill to **Andromeda Botanic Gardens** (daily 9am–5pm), run by the Barbados National Trust. On a cliff overlooking the east coast, Andromeda's 6 acres (2.4ha) of blooms and shrubs represent one of the finest collections in the region. The garden was developed in 1954 by the late horticulturist Iris Bannochie as her weekend retreat. Eventually she opened it to the public and as she developed the gardens and acquired specimens from around the world, they became a major attraction. In 1988 she bequeathed the estate to the people of Barbados.

The property is tastefully landscaped with ponds, three waterfalls, streams, shady nooks, rocky ledges, and marvelous splashes of color. The orchid collection is vast, and because of the tremendous variety there is almost always something in bloom. Andromeda also has one of the most extensive collections of hibiscus and

Top: Chalky Mount architecture
Right: coastal contrasts in Bathsheba

other flowering shrubs in the Caribbean, and the succulents are virtually a garden in themselves. Visitors are given guide sheets to enable them to identify the various species.

To make your way home, continue up the hill, turn right and travel back the way you came, or go on to explore St George and St John.

9. THE ST GEORGE VALLEY
AND ST JOHN *(see map, p52)*

A day tour through the countryside. Visit important historic sites including St George's Parish Church, Francia Plantation House, Gun Hill Signal Station, Orchid World, and St John's Parish Church. Stop off at Codrington College for a walk along College nature trail, then to Bath, St John, on the Atlantic coast for a swim and a bite to eat.

Take the ABC Highway to the Norman Niles roundabout (between Hothersal and 'Bussa') and follow the road briefly to the Salters turn-off on the left – you will see the signs for Salters and Gun Hill. Stay on this road until you meet a crossroads (Charles Rowe Bridge) with a petrol station, then turn right. In a few hundred yards we come to **St George's Parish Church**, the island's oldest parish church. Destroyed in the 1780 hurricane and rebuilt in 1784 (it survived the 1831 Great Hurricane), St George's is a blend of Georgian and Gothic styles. It has the distinction of housing the spectacular Benjamin West painting of the Resurrection (over the altar).

Continue up the hill to **Francia Plantation House**, a Barbadian planter's home which was built in 1913. The descendants of the original owner maintained and lived in the mansion until it was sold and closed to the public. The gardens include fountains, ferns, and manicured lawns.

From Francia follow the route up Gun Hill to the signed entrance to **Gun Hill Signal Station** (Mon–Sat 9am–5pm). Built in 1818, Gun Hill served not only as a signal station, communicating with the Christ Church and St Joseph stations, but also as a convalescence facility for soldiers and their families, for the strong winds that sweep through this area kept it free of the dreaded yellow fever-carrying mosquitoes.

The site's landscaped gardens and the sweeping south coast panorama make this a favorite stop for visitors – and so it was almost 150 years ago, when the historian Schomburgk wrote in his *History of Barbados*, '...no stranger who visits Barbados should omit to see this spot.'

The landmark coral stone lion, carved in 1868 by Captain Henry Wilkinson with the assistance of four military laborers, stands 7ft (2m) tall. The Latin inscription at the base comes from Psalm 72, Verse 8: 'He shall have dominion also from sea to sea and from river unto the end of the earth' (alluding, it is thought, to British dominion over the island). On a cliff top 700ft (213m) above sea level, the sculpture affectionately known as the 'lion at Gun Hill,' was restored by the Barbados National Trust in 1983.

Continuing on Highway 3B you pass through one of the lushest districts on the island and, depending on the time of year, you will see cane growing or being harvested. If you have an interest in horticulture, stop at **Orchid World** (daily 9am–5pm). Take a self-guided tour along the meandering pathways of these spectacular gardens with waterfalls, rock gardens, coral grottos, and 20,000 beautiful orchids.

Back on Highway 3B take a left turn at Four Roads (crossroads) and follow the signs to the beautifully restored **Villa Nova**, a former plantation house that was once the home of British Prime Minister Sir Anthony Eden. The property, which has also been a country hotel, is in a tranquil spot and is furnished with quality antiques.

Return to Four Roads, but this time turn left at the crossroads, and continue straight on to St John's Parish Church. Remain on this road, driving straight through Four Roads (past the fire station) and keep going. You will soon see **St John's Parish Church**, on a cliff, straight ahead of you.

A Byzantine Tomb

The church only dates back to 1836 – previous churches on the site were destroyed by hurricanes – but its centuries-old churchyard and surroundings are a treat for history buffs and even the mildly curious. Old tombstones with bizarre inscriptions populate this graveyard. The most notable belongs to Ferdinando Paleologus, buried here in 1670, a descendant of the brother of the last Byzantine Emperor, Constantine the Great. He fought as a Royalist in the English Civil War and after 1645 came as a refugee to Barbados where his family owned land. He served as St John's churchwarden for several years.

Left: Francia Plantation House. **Top:** the island's oldest parish church, St George's. **Right:** the lion at Gun Hill

The church itself is a well-appointed, solidly-built Gothic-style structure. Its magnificent interior includes a beautifully crafted spiraling staircase and pulpit, carved from six different woods: ebony, locust, local mahogany and machineel, and imported oak and pine. The church also has a beautiful sculpture carved by Sir Richard Westmacott, sculptor of the Lord Nelson statue that still stands in the center of Bridgetown.

Even the view from the churchyard is lovely, capturing a sweeping east coast panorama from an 800-ft (244-m) escarpment. There is also a small drinks and souvenir shop on the property.

College of Divinity

Coming out of St John's, turn left for Codrington College. Just past St John primary school turn left again and drive down the hill (Coach Hill), a steep, winding descent that provides tantalizing glimpses of the pristine coast. When you reach the bottom (Sergeant Street), continue on to the right and **Codrington College** (daily 10am–4pm; admission charge) is only a few minutes' drive from here on the left-hand side. Tall cabbage palms line the lane through the entrance; you will see the lily pond on your left and the college directly in front of you.

The college was founded by Christopher Codrington, a visionary and benefactor of the poor in Barbados, who was born on the estate in 1668 and died in the original mansion, now the Principal's Lodge, in 1710. Though a sugar planter by profession, his views and philosophy were very different from those of the other plantation owners of the day. In his will he stipulated that his estate of 800 acres (323ha) be overseen by the Anglican missionary organization, the Society for the Propagation of the Gospel, in order to establish a facility of divinity and general education for the children of African slaves – a revolutionary idea at that time. In fact the bequest was never followed according to Codrington's wishes, but instead educated wealthier boys to prepare them for Codrington (Theology) College.

The college buildings were constructed in 1743 and opened as Codrington Grammar School in 1745. It became a university level institution in

1830 and in 1875 gained its affiliation to the University of Durham, England, offering degrees from that institution. Since 1965 Codrington College has been part of the University of the West Indies and is the theological college of the Anglican Church for the West Indies Province.

The path to inner tranquillity and peace is reflected in the grounds and buildings of this institution, from the wonderful views and the serenity of the lily pond to the architecture of the college and the artifacts it holds. The college chapel is especially beautiful, with its glass mosaic of the Good Shepherd above an altar made of several native woods, including ebony.

Left: a watery view of Codrington College

The college's nature trail, which is well marked, is a pleasant walk (short and on the flat) that begins by the lily pond and leads through the bamboo stand and into a wooded area. The flora is numbered and identified in the college brochure.

Bath and Breathtaking Views

To continue to Bath, go back towards Coach Hill, then turn right down the hill just past where the road heads back up Coach Hill. A few hundred yards ahead are the remnants of an old sugar factory. Turn right here and follow the road to **Bath**. There is a large car park, toilet facilities, a snack bar, and a beach with a lifeguard. This is generally a safe place to have a swim, but as a precaution ask first and stay to the left where the bottom is sandier.

There are picnic tables nestled under shade trees, and if you feel like another short walk you can follow the car park to its end where a dirt road leads to more beach houses. Follow this lane and turn uphill on the path just after the bridge, where there is a small waterfall. You can continue turning uphill or keep straight along. The little path meanders along the coastline as far as Martin's Bay.

If you prefer a 'rum shop' snack, when you come out of Bath there are a couple of places at the base of Coach Hill on Sergeant Street where you can purchase delicious fresh baked breads and sandwich fillers. Heading home you can go back the way you came or opt for the adventurous route, taking Highway 4. In taking the latter route, you can make one last stop for a breathtaking view of the entire southeast coastline. Leaving Bath, turn left by the old smoke stack and go back towards Codrington College. Turn right immediately after the college and go up Society Hill. Turn right at the top and drive through Codrington High School's grounds and park by the Holy Cross church. Here you will get a special view of the southeastern end of the island as well as a closer look at a local private school, which has one of the nicest locations on the island.

To get on Highway 4 come back to the road and continue on to the junction (Society Plantation). Turn left and follow the road to the junction (at the petrol station). Turn right and you are on Highway 4. While this route twists a bit at first, once on the highway, it is a pastoral drive which leads you back to your starting point.

Above: a lifeguard keeps watch
Right: on the beach

The Southern Seaboard

10. THE BUSTLING SOUTH COAST (see map, p60)

This is a straightforward coastal drive from Hastings to Silver Sands. The south coast is a hub of commercial activity and nightlife so you may want to visit the St Lawrence area, on another occasion, in the evening. There are lots of shopping opportunities, restaurants, and beach stops.

West coast visitors should take the ABC Highway through the Pine, where you will see the CBC satellite dish on the left after the first set of traffic lights. Follow the road to the next lights, and on your left you will see the Barbados External Telecommunications (BET) office. Continue to the third set of traffic lights and turn left. Get in the right-hand lane to exit on the far right at the next roundabout to the start of Rendezvous Hill. When you reach the bottom of the hill, turn right at the lights to reach Highway 7. For

those of you based on the south coast, join this tour at your leisure. This route involves doubling back, so if you see something that grabs your interest you can have a closer look on the return trip.

In **Hastings**, an old military outpost, there are a number of sights worth visiting. Notice the red brick guard wall and buildings that are now primarily a residential complex. This is Pavilion Court, home of the **Mallalieu Motor Collection**. This selection of vintage cars includes a 1937 Chevrolet and a Bentley.

The stately white Savannah Hotel opposite was one of the early Barbadian hotels and first opened as the Sea View in 1889. Just past it is a small road that goes down to the Amaryllis Beach Resort, and a lovely beach with shallow sea pools, perfect for young children.

From here work your way back towards Rendezvous. The length of this coast is packed with banks, shopping plazas, and eateries. Among the more interesting plazas is **Quayside**, on the left opposite Rockley Beach Park.

Rockley to Worthing

The plaza is a great place to 'lime,' or hang out and watch the world go by. Have a coffee at the **Italia Doro** coffee house, or go to **Patisserie Flindt** for its world class cakes and pastries. Across the road at **Rockley Beach Park** is Accra beach, where there is a paved car park and kiosks for the beach vendors, loungers and parasols are available to rent, and services include life guards and rangers. The beach here is beautiful with a gentle surf which

Above: there are water sports galore

makes it a popular spot. You can usually find a coconut vendor – it is remarkable and sometimes quite alarming to watch how swiftly the coconuts are sliced open with a sharp machete. Try some refreshing coconut water straight from the coconut. As the coconuts mature the water or milk forms a jelly which is delicious, but in very mature nuts there is no liquid – just the familiar hard white lining of the coconut flesh.

Continue on Highway 7, passing Rendezvous, and take the third right turn after **Sandy Bay Beach Club** by the Chinese restaurant. This tiny avenue will lead you to a glorious stretch of sand known as **Sandy Beach**. There is a natural lagoon here that provides particularly safe bathing for children and the protective reef can be explored at low tide. The strong breeze here, not typical of west coast beaches, keeps it at a pleasant temperature, but beware, there is little shade here. Chairs and sun umbrellas can be rented for the day. If you are hungry, sample the good value fare at the relaxed **Carib Beach Bar**; they also have showers and live entertainment.

On leaving the Carib, turn right onto the main road and almost immediately on your left is the entrance to the **Graeme Hall Nature Sanctuary** (daily 8am–6pm) on the island's last remaining coastal wetland and mangrove swamp. It is a natural roosting and breeding ground for migratory birds, most notably egrets. It has become a distinguished birdwatching site with a walk-through aviary and interpretive center. Here you can visit the Gully Habitat, Marshland, Migrating Bird and St Vincent Amazon aviaries and follow a boardwalk-signed trail across the swamp. You can also stop for a drink and a snack overlooking the lake.

St Lawrence Gap to Oistins

The next right turn is into **St Lawrence Gap**. This one-way strip wakes up at night with its bars, clubs and restaurants. Our stop is the **Chattel House Village**, well into the Gap on the left, a cluster of chattel house-style shops with local arts,

Top: on the beach at Worthing
Right: fun for children

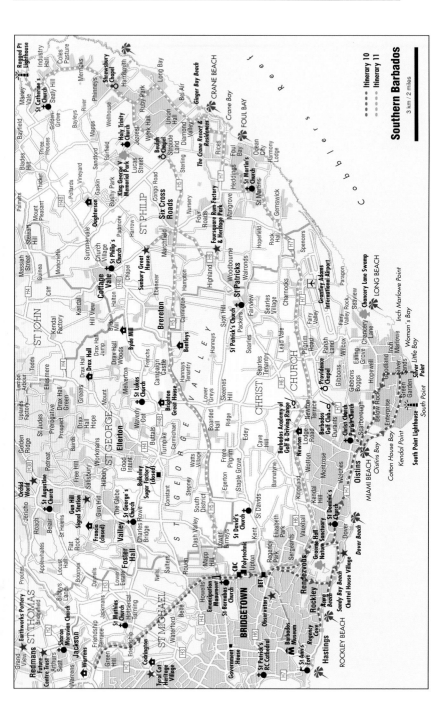

crafts, and souvenirs. These shops are similar in design, but not in content, to the Holetown chattel village. Also worth a stop is **Caribbean Walkers World**, with a range of locally-made and imported Caribbean craft items. If you are ready for a snack, a good choice is **Bean-n-Bagel** (Mon–Fri 7am–4pm), which also has internet facilities.

On the weekend 'The Gap', as it is known locally, is the ideal place to hang out in the bars and clubs, but there are activities during the week too. The After Dark nightclub has DJ music every night and has also been the venue of a weekly colorful cultural dance show. There are a variety of bars including McBride's and Jumby's, and for a touch of Miami style there is Pravda, a classy cocktail bar located at the beginning of The Gap.

Follow St Lawrence Gap to its end, passing Dover Convention Center and various hotels, until you reach Highway 7, where you turn right. Next stop is **Oistins**, where you can visit the fish market on the right in the center of town. If you have cooking facilities in your accommodation, you might want to buy some 'boned' flying fish. Barbadians have made quite a skill of filleting this slender fish, transforming it into a staple dish. They are quick and easy to steam or grill, but are most typically eaten fried. The fish market is a hive of activity in season with a bevy of 'boners,' hawkers, and 'cleaners' all busily working. The best time to visit is around 4pm when the fishermen return with the catch of the day, which can include dorado, snapper, kingfish and even shark. At weekends – particularly Friday nights when there is the **Oistins Fish Fry** – the market area is packed until late with party-goers and revelers, and music blares out of every rum shop and stall. Oistins is primarily a fishing town and, while there is little else of interest here, the small fishing boats and market make it well worth seeing.

Beyond Oistins

From Oistins take the right exit when you reach the fork in the road, turn right again, and at the T-junction turn left. (If you choose to turn right instead you will come to **Miami Beach/Enterprise Beach**, which is a peaceful, scenic beach stop.)

Follow the road or take the right turn that loops into the fancy Atlantic Shores residential area. The **South Point Lighthouse** is in the center of the housing area. Because of the extensive development, driving through this area can be confusing. Follow the road inland, through twists and turns, until a church with a green roof appears on the right. Turn right, down the hill into **Silver Sands**. Keep loosely to the coast, taking the first left turn and following the signs to Silver Rock, our lunch stop.

Silver Point Hotel offers inexpensive, hearty local fare in a laid-back gazebo-style beach restaurant, from where you can watch the windsurfers in the waves. Top international professional and amateur windsurfers practice here,

Right: filleting flying fish

many staying the whole season from January to May, and international competitions are held here in January. If you are inclined to do some windsurfing yourself, Silver Rock Windsurf Shop is next door to the restaurant. Owned and operated by renowned windsurfer Brian Talma, this is a well stocked shop and the best place to pick up advice. Talma also runs a **Windsurfing Academy** by the Silver Point Hotel.

To return home, drive back up the hill passing the church with the green roof, continue straight on to the roundabout. Take the first exit and follow the road which will take you back to Oistins.

11. ST PHILIP *(see map, p60)*

This full-day tour includes visits to Sunbury Great House, a traditional plantation home dating back to the 1660s, and the Rum Factory and Heritage Park at Foursquare, before making a beach stop at the little known Harrismith Beach and venturing on to view Ragged Point Lighthouse. Return via one of the island's most historic hotels, The Crane Beach Hotel, with its stunning view.

Although there are a number of refreshment options on this route, having a packed lunch in one of the picturesque coves is particularly pleasant.

To get to the first stop join the ABC Highway and travel to the Emancipation Statue roundabout. Take the Mapp Hill exit (Highway 5) to the east. After a 10-minute drive the road forks – veer left and enjoy this lengthy drive through the lush fields of St George. Ten more minutes along the road, look out for the sign for Sunbury and a left turn (just before Six Cross Roads). The entrance to the property is on your left.

Sunbury Great House (daily 9am–5pm) dates back to the 1660s. The entire house is open for viewing, each room impeccably furnished and decorated according to the period. This is a true plantation house tour that gives a sense of the lifestyle and living standards of the elite planter class in those early days. There is an extensive collection of old prints, china, glassware, and antiques, as well as the region's largest assortment of horse-drawn carriages. You can roam into the gardens and surrounding wooded area and stop for a snack in the courtyard café.

Park and Paintings

From Sunbury return along the same road, this time continuing straight on across the junction with Highway 5. At the next junction turn right for the entrance to the Rum Factory and Heritage Park, shortly on your left.

The **Heritage Park and Foursquare Rum Distillery** (Mon–Fri 9am–5pm; admission charge) at Foursquare opened in November 1996, the brainchild of well-known local businessman and rum producer David Seale. A well-planned 9-acre (3.6ha) site encompassing culture, art, shopping, history and rum production, it offers several hours entertainment. The entry fee allows visitors the complete run of the park and factory.

On the complex you will find the **Art Foundry**, a gallery housed in a beautiful 250-year old building, where you can see permanent and visiting art displays. There are also six shops, a Folk Museum depicting traditional Barbadian life in the 1950s and '60s, a full bar, and a snackbar available for refreshment. The Cane Pit Amphitheatre is the venue for shows, concerts, and other events (call ahead for a schedule, tel: 420-1977).

The property, which dates back some 350 years, was originally a working plantation, then a sugar factory was erected around 1730, later becoming Foursquare Sugar Factory, which operated until 1988. Remnants of the factory and its machinery pepper the complex, in the form of creatively designed furniture in the Art Foundry and more formal displays in the outdoor sugar factory museum. Here the owners tell the story of sugar amid shady trees and a children's play area.

Factory relics can also be seen on the tour of what is the region's most energy-efficient rum distillery, a computerized state-of-the-art distillery that is the most modern in the world. As you follow the distilling process you will come to a 'fire wall,' a remnant of the original factory, where you can get a glimpse of what sugar making was like 300 years ago.

Coves and Cliffs

For a swim at the delightful **Harrismith Beach**, turn right at the main gate of the park and drive to Six Cross Roads (actually a roundabout) along Highway 6. Take the fourth exit, passing Chefette (a popular fast-food restaurant specializing in fried chicken and roti, a local favorite) to your right. Follow this road for several minutes. Shortly after the sign for Mike's Trading on your right you will come to a sharp S-bend. Go down the secondary road instead of finishing the bend. Stay on this road to its end, then park and descend to the magnificent beach on foot. It is a long walk to this isolated, idyllic cove, so be prepared.

Top: Barbadian chattel house
Left: the beach at Long Bay

This coastline has some of the most attractive bays on the island and a few beaches that are picture postcard perfect, and often empty. Back on the road and on the way to the abandoned **Ragged Point Lighthouse** you may want to sample **Bottom Bay**, a little further up the coast from Harrismith; look for the signpost. Continue on the main road past several villages until the lighthouse appears in the distance. Turn right at the Marley Vale sign and you come to the lighthouse road; you can drive right up to the building. This picturesque spot is worth exploring. Walk around the lighthouse

and the ruins and follow the footpath to the windswept cliffs for awe-inspiring views on both sides. The lighthouse used to warn mariners away from the dangerous Cobbler's Reef on the southeast coast.

The lighthouse marks the easternmost point of the island of Barbados, where the scenery becomes more desolate and the coastline is spectacularly buffeted by strong Atlantic waves.

Pirate's Point

South of Harrismith, along the coast is an old hotel, **Sam Lord's Castle**, and below it the white sand of **Long Bay**. This once splendid Georgian-style mansion is steeped in history and folklore, however, the hotel is closed.

Sam Lord's was built in the 1820s by the infamous Samuel Hall Lord, a purported pirate and generally nefarious character. He was said to trick passing ships on to the surrounding reefs in order to plunder them. The castle was one of the finest edifices on the island and an example of the extravagant excesses of its period, with elaborate crystal chandeliers, and plaster centerpieces decorating the ceilings. British architect Charles Rutter, who once worked on Windsor Castle, was responsible for much of the interior woodwork and plasterwork. With the help of two Italians, it took Rutter almost four years to complete. Standing on 72 acres (29ha) of land with fruit trees and shrubs, the building changed hands several times and eventually became an integral part of a vacation resort, which went out of business in 2004.

Continuing along the road to the **Crane Resort and Residences**, simply called the Crane, drive along the straight from Sam Lord's to the main junction and turn left. Follow this road around a sharp right bend, passing the Crane Beach signpost, and continue for several minutes to the luxury resort's main entrance on your left.

Above: a view of Ragged Point Lighthouse
Right: gone fishing

Cliff Top Views at the Crane

This lovely old hotel was a plantation house in the mid-1700s. The main mansion, **Marine Villa**, has been carefully restored but it maintains its original features forming part of the hotel's east block, it is thought to have been built around 1790, possibly by Sam Lord before he built his castle. The building was converted into a hotel in 1887 and is one of the oldest on Barbados. In fact, one of its first famous guests in the 1890s was American cowboy 'Wild Bill' Hickock. Its romantic setting, perched on the cliff overlooking the turbulent Atlantic, has made it a haven for honeymooners. The hotel, which stands on 40 acres (16ha) of land is expanding at a rapid rate with five-story blocks of luxury apartments being built along the cliff top near the original hotel. Developments also include a spa, a beach bar in the coconut grove and a glass elevator that will transport guests down the cliff to the beach below. The Crane has an à la carte lunch menu (daily 12.30–3pm; service is typically slow) and live music; on Sunday there is a popular buffet lunch.

The Crane's wide beach of fine powdery sand is one of the island's finest, and it enjoys the benefit of a protective reef that keeps turbulent undertows at bay. The front coral-stone steps leading down to the beach are no longer in use, but they are said to have been hand-carved in the 1700s. Just south of the property is the 'Horse,' a secret bathing spot for women in the 1700s. The steps, cut out of the cliffs, are still there, though the pool, which is wedged between the coral ledges, is not as placid as it was then.

To head home, turn left at the main entrance and keep following the winding course of this road past St Martin's church. After the sharp right bend by a stand of mahogany trees, veer left at the junction and continue past the airport, joining the highway at the second roundabout (right exit).

Continue home on the highway or take the turn-off at the first (Chickmont) roundabout and head to the **Barbados Academy of Golf** (daily 8am–11pm; tel: 420-7405), at Balls Complex. Also here is **Ocean Park** (daily 9am–6pm), a marine aquarium featuring freshwater falls, a living reef display, touch pool, ray pool, and a sea-rescue area.

Above: dry dock

Leisure Activities

SHOPPING

Barbados is no bargain basement, but you can find duty-free goods and local souvenirs at reasonable prices.

Duty Free

Barbados abounds in duty-free shopping. There are many small shops and department store branches in the tourist hubs, but the widest selection by far is on Broad Street, Bridgetown's main street. Large department stores and specialty shops cram both sides of the street, offering everything from the world's finest china and electronic equipment to cashmere sweaters and internationally known skin-care products and toiletries.

With a bit of advance research, you might find items well below prices charged at home. However, duty-free does not automatically mean cheaper. If you have ideas about particular items that you would like to shop for, it is always sensible to check your home country prices first. Depending on the goods and where you are from, you may find what you want cheaper at home.

The bigger, multistory department stores in Bridgetown are **Cave Shepherd** and **Harrisons**. Both have exhaustive (and exhausting) duty-free sections. Niche stores include **Colombian Emeralds International**, **Correia's**, **Little Switzerland** and the **Royal Shop**, which specialize in high quality jewelry. Little Switzerland also has an impressive range of camera and audio equipment.

You can only buy duty-free if you present your passport and return ticket, so don't forget to take them when shopping. You can take most items with you at the time of purchase, but you still have to pick up tobacco, alcohol, and a few other items at the airport. If you are staying in a west or south coast hotel Cave Shepherd operates a free shopping shuttle into Bridgetown and back. It picks up around 9am, 11am and 2.30pm, depending on numbers. It's best to book the day before, although you can try on the day, tel: 431 2078, 8.30am–4pm.

Rum

The island is vastly experienced in rum production so you will find wide selections and excellent value for money just about anywhere, including duty-free shops, virtually all tourist shopping centers, and even in the supermarkets.

Rum products range from 'white' or clear rums to very dark rums, and from 'young' rums to well-aged. There are also specialty rum products, such as Malibu (white rum with coconut), as well as rum brandies and creams. Principal local names include Mount Gay, which operates the world's oldest distillery, established in 1703, Cockspur, Doorly's, and a white rum line from E. S. A Field, a subsidiary of Doorly's. Each line has a number of products based on age, color, and proof; watch your labels, as a few of these rums go heavily into 'overproof.'

Arts and Crafts

Barbados is blossoming with local artists and there are several private galleries that offer a good sampling of what is around. In many instances you may be able to contact a local artist directly. The best known – and most commercial – outlet is the **Best of Barbados** chain of shops, offering an entire line of mass-produced items imprinted with the works of Jill Walker.

For more personal tastes, you can view a wide range of work at the **Barbados Arts Council** shop in the Pelican Craft Center, on Harbour Road just outside Bridgetown. This cluster of shops is also a fruitful source of handicrafts in wood, coral, and other media.

There are many other private galleries, including the **Verandah Gallery** (the Old

Left: dining outdoors
Right: local pottery decorated with a flying fish

Spirit Bond Mall, Bridgetown), reflecting local and regional culture, and lifestyle; **Mango's**, in Speightstown features silk screens by Michael Adams; **Gang of 4 Art Studio**, also in Speightstown, and **The Art Foundry** at Heritage Park. The artist Vanita Comissiong, runs **On the Wall** gallery at Earthworks in St Thomas and displays her own and the work of other regional artists at Champers Restaurant, Christ Church.

For locally produced handicrafts, **Pelican Craft Center** on Harbour Road just outside Bridgetown, sells basketry, woodwork, jewelry, and more; or try the **Chattel House Village** in St Lawrence Gap. By far the best collection of arts and crafts can be found at local fairs and festivals. Scan the press for current events.

Mahogany is a slow-growing tropical hardwood that has beautiful texture and color. **Medford Craft Village**, located just north of Bridgetown, is a shopping expedition in itself. You'll find just about everything that can possibly be fashioned from mahogany and other woods, and you can watch the workers shaping the products on the spot. If you're not able to get to

Medford's, a limited range of their products are found in most tourist shops.

For batik a good bet is **John C Mayers Batik**, Bathsheba, St Joseph. Other hand-painted art works, mostly in the form of clothing, can be purchased from **Colours of de Caribbean** in Bridgetown. Look out for locally produced swimsuits from **Sandbox Designs** and hand-painted soft furnishings under the **Mango Jam** label.

For pottery, **Earthworks** in Edgehill

Heights, St Thomas sells tableware and household items that reflect Caribbean style. **Painted Earth** features unusual hand-painted ceramics which can also be found at **The Monkey Pot** shops in the Pelican Craft Center and St Lawrence Gap.

Antiques

Antiques shops dot the shopping areas, especially around Holetown. While fascinating to browse through, for the most part items in these stores are grossly overpriced. But you just might find a quaint curio in your price-range. An antiques shop worth trying is **La Gallerie Antique** just outside Holetown.

T-shirts

The T-shirt industry thrives on Barbados. Many items are made from the silkier textured sea island cotton, and quality is generally high. Try **Irie Blue** and **Ganzee** stores, or **Cave Shepherd**.

Bajan Delicacies

If you enjoy spicy Barbadian cuisine then why not take a bottle of hot pepper sauce or Bajan seasoning back home? Sauces and seasonings are cheapest in the supermarkets, but they can also be found individually or in gift packages in souvenir shops.

Above: Medford mahogany
Above Right: fresh fruit. **Right**: stopping for some liquid refreshment.

EATING OUT

The long-standing British influence, coupled with a subsistence diet based primarily on ground provisions, kept Barbados almost bereft of creative culinary flair for centuries. But tourism attracted international-class chefs and brought overseas training for locals, and these two developments helped alter the face of Barbados' menus. Creative cuisine now abounds, and the emphasis is on the use of local ingredients to make award-winning dishes.

The national dish is flying fish and *cou cou*. Flying fish is wholly Barbados' own. Small and quite delicate and tasty when not overcooked or too heavily seasoned, it is served many ways, including fried, steamed, and roasted. *Cou cou*, an adaptation of the West African 'foo-foo' vegetable dish, is a side dish of mashed corn meal (or breadfruit) and okra, beaten until smooth.

The lamb of the indigenous black belly sheep is finding its way onto restaurant menus, usually fried, baked, or grilled. Its gamy flavor and prime lean cuts attract a growing appreciation.

Chicken is enjoyed in every form and fashion and is popular in *roti (see below)*. Other little side dishes include breadfruit, a starchy fruit often prepared like potatoes, but especially delicious pickled with peppers, onions, and lime. Plantain is a bananalike fruit that is sliced and most often fried. These 'fritters' have a slightly sweet flavor, yet are compatible with a savory meal.

Jug jug is available strictly at Christmas time, a local dish of ground pigeon peas flavored with port, which is a traditional favorite.

Macaroni pie is an unlikely but popular local staple. Barbadians prefer it solid with plenty of creamy cheese and tomato ketchup.

Pudding and souse, once known as a 'poor man's food,' is wholly Barbadian. Assumed to have come from the plantation days, they evolved into popular dishes traditionally eaten on Saturday. Puddings made from seasoned sweet potato stuffed into the pig's intestines and utilising the pig's blood, which is left out in the more common and widely available white steamed pudding. Souse is pickled pork, which uses only the pig's head and/or feet.

Roti is a folded wrap with a curry filling of chicken, beef, goat, shrimp, or vegetable usually combined with potato.

Steak fish is popular, especially king fish, dolphin (not the 'Flipper' kind, but dorado) and several several types of 'red' fish, such as snapper, that is grilled, blackened, or fried. Dishes vary depending on the season.

Local grog

It is often said that it is cheaper to drink than eat in Barbados. The island shines in the drinks arena, particularly beverages that utilize rum or rum products. Favorites include the age-old rum punch or Planter's punch, a very smooth drink with a surprising kick, so beware. The recipe calls for 'one sour' (lime), 'two sweet' (sugar), 'three strong' (rum) and 'four weak' (water). Punch à creme is a Christmas favorite, using eggs, milk, rum, and bitters. Also at Christmas you may hear about Falernum, a traditional drink made from lime and white rum, which is boiled to a syrupy consistency then bottled and fermented. Also at Christmas you may

hear about 'corn 'n' oil,' which is a traditional drink made with rum and Falernum.

Mauby, a bark soaked in spices, is an acquired taste, with bite. More appealing perhaps is ginger beer, made from ginger and lime. While it can be bought bottled, it is often homemade. Sorrel is a spicy traditional Christmas drink: the dried sepals of the sorrel plant are steeped in spices such as cinnamon and cloves and served with or without rum added.

The island's best known beer is Banks, which has won international awards. Coconut water is available in some bars, but also from roadside vendors, who will cut your coconut for you and serve it with a straw. They will also slash open the coconut if you want the 'jelly' – the soft part that is just beginning to solidify. Another thirst quencher is cane juice, taken from sugar cane. Available only during harvest season.

RESTAURANTS

There are nearly as many places to eat on Barbados as there are places to stay. But bear in mind that many ingredients are imported or, when not available, substitutions are made, so not all foreign cuisines are entirely authentic. But Barbados has something special: a bevy of international-class chefs. While most are found in the finer hotels, others have opened their own restaurants.

Barbados is not a cheap place to dine out. While it has many fast food eateries along

the south and west coasts, even these can run high – and not very fast, either. But there are good, value-for-money fast food establishments to be found, and when it comes to economical dining the south coast reigns.

This selection is by no means complete (*see Nightlife, page 74* for other choices). For a guide to prices (in US dollars per person, meal only) including 15 percent tax: Inexpensive ($) = under $20; Moderate ($$) = $20–40; Expensive ($$$) = $40–60.

Bridgetown

Ideal if you are in town for shopping or business. Restaurants in Bridgetown are usually good value and the service is quite quick. Many of the capital's restaurants are only open on regular shopping days for lunch between 10am and 3pm.

The Balcony Restaurant & Beer Garden
Cave Shepherd, 1st Floor, Broad Street
Tel: 431-2088
Cafeteria-style restaurant, with an emphasis on light, healthy meals. Daily specials and salad bar. Lunch only. $

Big John's
Broad Street
No phone
Bajan specialties such as ribs, macaroni pie and roti. A drive-through location at Hastings Plaza, with parking and some seating. $

Chefette
Branches on Upper and Lower Broad Street, Marhill Street, and Harbour Road
Tel: 430-3300
Largest local fast food chain. Four locations in the city, drive-through facility at Harbour Road. Lunch and dinner. $

Mustor's
McGregor Street
Tel: 426-5175
Bajan food, no frills. Lunch only. $

Waterfront Café
Bridgetown Marina, The Careenage
Tel: 427-0093
A dockside café overlooking the city, a local favorite, serving Caribbean and continental dishes. Daily specials. Lunch and dinner.

Above: preparing sorrel

Live entertainment, known on the island for its hot jazz nights. $$

Bridgetown Environs

Avoid the bustle of the city in a bistro or restaurant on the outskirts. You will generally pay a bit more, but the atmosphere is relaxing. Make reservations where possible.

The Boatyard
Bay Street, St Michael
Tel: 436-2622
A bubbling bistro atmosphere with beach facilities close to town. Live late-night entertainment. Friday evening happy hours. $$

The Boucan
Savannah Hotel, Hastings
Tel: 434-3827
Hearty buffet and a la carte. A delicious mix of Caribbean and International dishes. $$

Brown Sugar
Aquatic Gap, off Bay Street
Tel: 426-7684
Delicious Caribbean dishes, with value-for-money buffet lunch. A la carte dinner. $–$$

Lobster Alive
Bay Street
Tel: 435-0305
Fresh Grenadine lobster flown in every day. Beach front setting with umbrellas available. $$

West Coast

This is the gold coast of Barbados where dining is at its best and prices go hand in hand. Along this coast is a selection of elegant restaurants, bistros, and bars.

Blue Monkey
Paynes Bay, St James
Tel: 432-7528
A west coast beach bar and restaurant with a lively atmosphere and creative dishes. Daily specials. $–$$

Calabaza
Prospect, St James
Tel: 424-4557
Spectacular oceanfront setting and friendly atmosphere make this a popular choice.

Exquisite cuisine and great service. Reservations recommended. $$–$$$

The Cliff
Derricks, St James
Tel: 432-1922
One of the island's finest restaurants, with innovative food and terraced seating overlooking the ocean. Truly elegant service and style. For an extra special treat. Reservations recommended. $$$

Cocomos
Holetown, St James
Tel: 432-0134
A bistro on the beach, with colorful decor. Lots of Caribbean flavor. Daily specials. $$

The Fish Pot
Little Good Harbour, St Peter
Tel: 439-2604
Caribbean and International cuisine served in stylish surroundings, on the oceanfront. Specialties include seafood crepes and spicy curries. Breakfast, lunch and dinner. $$–$$$

Fisherman's Pub
Speightstown, St Peter
Tel: 422-2703
One of the better beachside rum shops and grills in the heart of Speightstown. Lunch and dinner. Lively and popular spot. $

Right: dining al fresco

La Mer
Port St Charles, St Peter
Tel: 419-2000
Excellent cuisine such as grilled meats and fish dishes served in a beautiful lagoon setting. Popular Sunday brunch. Reservations recommended. $$–$$$

Lone Star
Mount Standfast, St James
Tel: 419-0599
Imaginative cuisine from balti to beluga caviar. Extensive wine list. Lunch and dinner. Reservations recommended. $$–$$$

Mango's by the Sea
Speightstown, St Peter
Tel: 422-0704
Inviting oceanfront restaurant. Good food and friendly staff. Daily specials. Dinner only. $$

The Mews
2nd Street, Holetown, St James
Tel: 432-1122
Balcony and courtyard dining, friendly service and gourmet European dishes. Dinner only. Reservations required. $$–$$$

Olives Bar & Bistro
2nd Street, Holetown, St James
Tel: 432-2112
A cosy bistro and lounge at the heart of Holetown, popular with locals. Mediterranean and Caribbean food. Daily specials. Dinner only. Reservations recommended. $$–$$$

Patisserie Flindt
1st Street, Holetown, St James
Tel: 432-2626
Charming garden café in the heart of Holetown. Breakfast, lunch, and tea. $

Sitar Indian Restaurant
2nd Street, Holetown, St James
Tel: 432-2248
Authentic East Indian cuisine in a comfortable setting. Dinner only. $$–$$$

The Tides Restaurant
Balmore House, Holetown
Tel: 432-8356
An elegant seaside setting. International dishes with a Caribbean flavor. $$$

South Coast
Best known for its nightlife, the south coast also has every type of dining experience. Expect to pay less than on the west.

Aqua
Main Road, Hastings, Christ Church
Tel: 420-2995
Stylish oceanfront restaurant with a creative menu: Bajan and Oriental. Reservations. $$$

Bean-n-Bagel Internet Café
Dover, Christ Church
Tel: 420-4604
A cozy café in the heart of the Gap. One of the few places open for a hearty breakfast of coffee and muffins. Internet access. $

Bellini's Trattoria
Little Bay Hotel, Corner St Lawrence Gap, Christ Church
Tel: 435-7246
A casual, quiet seaside Italian restaurant serving fresh pastas, seafood, and gourmet pizzas. Daily specials. Dinner only. $$

Bubba's Sports Bar
Rockley, Christ Church
Tel: 435-6217
American-style sports bar. Popular with local families. Breakfast, lunch, and dinner. $–$$

Top: frying in a buckpot

eating out   *73*

eating out

Café Sol
St Lawrence Gap, Christ Church
Tel: 435-9531
A popular Tex-Mex bar and restaurant. You may not mind the slow service if you indulge in a jug of margarita. Two happy hours; 6–7pm and 10–11pm. Reservations. $–$$

Carib Beach Bar & Restaurant
2nd Avenue, Worthing, Christ Church
Tel: 435-8540
A busy beach bar with spectacular views of Sandy Beach and the ocean. Relaxed atmosphere, varied menu and live music at weekends. Lunch and dinner. $–$$

Champers Wine Bar & Restaurant
Skeetes Hill, Christ Church
Tel: 434-3463
An elegant seaside place with great ocean views and a delicious and imaginative menu. Daily specials. Reservations advised. Lunch and dinner. $$–$$$

Josef's
St Lawrence Gap, Christ Church
Tel: 420-7638
By far the finest restaurant in this area, with balcony, patio, and garden seating. Delicious European cuisine. Daily specials. Reservations required. Dinner only. $$–$$$

Lucky Horseshoe Saloon & Steakhouse
Worthing, Christ Church
Tel: 435-5825
The only 24-hour bar/restaurant in Barbados. Specializing in huge USDA premium steaks and a selection of beer. Friendly service and good value. Daily specials. $–$$

Luigi's Italian Restaurant
Dover Woods, Christ Church
Tel: 428-9218
Open nearly 40 years, a cozy, no frills authentic Italian restaurant. Delicious food and a warm atmosphere. Dinner only. $$

Mike's Bar & Restaurant
Coral House, Silver Sands, Christ Church
Tel: 428-8616
A rustic seaside bar/restaurant with all-you-can-eat buffet. Menu changes daily. Friendly. Reservations advised. Dinner only. $

Pisces
St Lawrence Gap, Christ Church
Tel: 435-6564
Romantic restaurant on the water's edge, local and international seafood dishes. Daily specials. Dinner only. Reservations. $$

East Coast

Restaurants are popping up all along the rugged eastern coast. They are busy, especially at weekends and for Sunday lunch. Not all are open every day so call ahead.

Atlantis Hotel
Bathsheba, St Joseph
Tel: 433-9445
A sleepy, fading seaside hotel restaurant famed for its Sunday buffets. Lunch. $–$$

L'Azure
The Crane Hotel, St Philip
Tel: 423-6220
On the cliffs overlooking a beautiful beach. Specialising in international cuisine and fresh local seafood. Daily specials. Reservations recommended. $$$

Bonito Bar
Bathsheba, St Joseph
Tel: 433-9034
A rustic surfing hangout serving mostly local fare. Buffet and sandwiches. Lunch only. $

The Cove
Atlantic Park, Cattlewash, St Joseph
Tel: 433-9495
Small family restaurant, varied menu features seafood and Caribbean cuisine in a warm atmosphere. Daily specials. Lunch only. $–$$

Naniki Restaurant
Suriname, (off Horse Hill), St Joseph
Tel: 433-1300
In a lush valley overlooking the coast, serving Caribbean delicacies made with mostly home grown organic foods. Lunch only. $$

Round House Inn Restaurant & Bar
Bathsheba, St Joseph
Tel: 433-9678
A landmark restaurant with a small but imaginative menu of local and international dishes. Live entertainment. Reservations. $–$$

NIGHTLIFE

Nightlife in Barbados is highly varied, and there is no shortage of things to do. Music runs the gamut, from country-and-western and 'oldies' to dub and soca. For many years the island was not especially well known for its musical prowess, but in the early 1990s several groups and artistes burst onto the regional and international scene simultaneously and now much of the Caribbean region follows Barbados' lead. You should be able to sample some of this fine island talent during your stay.

Many of the larger hotels provide floor shows, live music, and other local acts, entertainment often staged during dinner. However, if you want to get out and experience a bit more local flavor, then you will definitely be looking at a late-night experience. While you can have an early night and still have fun, unlike many of the other islands where the streets are practically empty after dinner, in Barbados the action doesn't start until 11pm, particularly on the south coast, where the fun goes on until the early morning.

An addition to traditional local nightlife is the 'sports bar,' with satellite television. In Worthing there is Bubba's, The Lucky Horseshoe Saloon, which is open 24-hours, and Bert's Bar at the Abbeville Hotel. Further up the coast is McBride's in St Lawrence Gap and on the west coast Crocodile's Den. *(see West Coast listings page 75).*

South Coast to Bridgetown

The south coast, particularly the St Lawrence Gap strip and a short Bay Street stretch just before Bridgetown, teems with action well into the small hours. You will find everything here from elaborate floor shows to outdoor fish fries, where people gather for an impromptu bite to eat.

Oistins Fish Fry

A crowded hot spot, particularly on Friday nights. The casual atmosphere, outdoor setting, and pumping music, coupled with delicious fresh fish and seafood (prepared while you wait, and at a fraction of the local restaurant price), attract locals and visitors into the early morning. Parking is at a premium, so plan to go early and stay late. Join in the activities from dancing to dominoes and other games. A good vantage point to view the proceedings is from the string of rum shops opposite the market. Live music during Oistins Fish Festival.

The Boatyard
Bay Street, Bridgetown
Tel: 436-2622
A popular drinking spot with live bands several nights a week. This is a large open-air complex that hosts a variety of events. Call ahead for a current schedule of what's on.

Café Sol
St Lawrence Gap, Christ Church
Tel: 420-7655
Lively Mexican-style bar and restaurant with salsa music and a Tex-Mex menu. Popular meeting place; perfect before hitting the clubs.

Club Xtreme
Worthing, Christ Church
Tel: 435-4455
Large, popular club with different theme nights. Resident and guest DJs playing the latest dance craze, hip hop, reggae, and calypso.

Harbour Lights
Bay Street, Bridgetown
Tel: 436-7225
A late-night hangout and dance spot attracting a young to early middle-age crowd. On Carlisle Bay beach, it has a pleasant open-air

Above: Bajan Roots & Rhythms show

setting, elevated dance floor and food. There is a DJ and sometimes live acts. Cover charges vary. Action doesn't start before 11pm.

McBride's
St Lawrence Gap, Christ Church
Tel: 420-7646
This lively Irish pub is packed most nights. It features DJ music and live acts; popular with 20-somethings and British visitors. Party-night on Thursday.

The Plantation Theatre: Bajan Roots & Rhythms
St Lawrence Main Road, Christ Church
Tel: 428-5048
A glittering cabaret performance of Caribbean music, culture and dance. Dine to the sounds of live steel band music and dance the night away with top local talent. Performances on Wednesday and Friday. Call for details.

Reggae Lounge
St Lawrence Gap, Christ Church
Tel: 435-6462
A rustic open-air nightclub. The bar is at the top entrance level and there are steps down to the dance floor. Occasionally hosts live reggae acts but has DJ music most nights.

The Ship Inn
St Lawrence Gap, Christ Church
Tel: 420-7447
This long-standing venue in the Gap sets the pace. It deftly sails a course between pub/restaurant and bar/nightclub. The Ship is the island's only place with live entertainment most nights and it showcases local talent.

Waterfront Café
The Careenage
Tel: 427-0093
Frequent jazz acts and steel pan music by night. Dress is a little more upmarket than in other south coast venues. Sit at one of the small tables on the pavement and take in the picturesque harbor, or take a spin around the dance floor.

West Coast
Lower key than the island's south coast, the west coast offers a more refined nightlife.

Coach House
Paynes Bay, St James
Tel: 432-1163
Styled on a typical English pub. Extensively refurbished, it hosts live bands and more.

Crocodile's Den
Payne's Bay, St James
Tel: 432-7625
The place to go very late at night or early in the morning! Your host, Harry Hinds, plays requests from his record collection.

The Elbow Room
2nd Street, Holetown, St James
Tel: 432-1927
A lively bar with delicious grilled food, served in relaxed open-air surroundings.

The Mews
Holetown, St James
Tel: 432-1122
Friday nights feature a local jazz duo; intimate atmosphere attracts an upmarket crowd.

Oasis Bar
1st Street, Holetown, St James
Tel: 419-0320
The after-dinner crowds gather at this cozy spot. Friday nights are busy and finish late, with the tiny dance floor often packed.

East Coast
Round House
Bathsheba, St Joseph
Tel: 433-9678
Rock, reggae, and jazz, good food too. Take a jacket – it's cool in the evening.

Left: enjoy the sound of the steel pan

CALENDAR OF EVENTS

Contact the Barbados Tourism Authority (BTA), tel: 427-2623, for further information on any of the events listed here.

January

The Barbados National Trust (BNT) launches its annual **Open House** program. Every Wednesday afternoon the Trust leads visitors into some of the island's most celebrated private homes not normally open to the public. They include the opulent, the architecturally unique, and the historical. The program runs until early April. Tel: 436-9033 for more information.

The Barbados Horticultural Society also hosts its **Open Gardens** program this month. Local enthusiasts open their private gardens to the public in the afternoons on one day a week. To find out where to go, tel: 428-5889.

Tropical ambience and an exciting mix of headliner names makes Barbados' annual **Paint It Jazz** festival a big hit. The five-day event during the second week of January features a marathon of concerts in both indoor and outdoor settings. Tel: 429-2084 or the BTA on 427-2623.

February

Barbados has a very active Horticultural Society. Each year it hosts a weekend **Flower Show and Competition** at its headquarters at Balls Plantation, Christ Church. The event showcases all manner of locally and regionally grown flora from massive displays to single plants. For details, tel: 428-5889.

A little over a week of festivities marks the landing of the first settlers in Barbados in the **Holetown Festival**, which hinges on the February 17 landing date. A packed slate of daily events ranges from free concerts to an open-air arts and crafts market. A fun, family-oriented, grass roots event.

Barbados Gold Cup Festival at the beginning of February is organised by the Barbados Turf Club. Call 426-3980 for details.

March/April

The Sandy Lane Barbados Gold Cup Race usually on the first weekend in March is the island's premier horseracing event. This 9-furlong invitational race attracts class 'A' horses from Barbados and neighboring islands. The event draws a large crowd, a celebratory atmosphere, and much pomp and ceremony.

Easter heralds the **Holder's Opera Season**, a popular three-week attraction. Internationally acclaimed singers and actors mingle with local performers in Shakespearean productions, operas, and special concerts in the outdoor setting of the Holders Plantation House. Deviating from the main musical theme, the program also embraces polo, golf, and cricket events.

Oistins Fish Festival, held in the fishing town of Oistins over the Easter Weekend, celebrates the island's fishing industry in a host of mainly free events, including a street fair and fish boning and other competitions highlighting fishing skills.

The **Royal Westmoreland Barbados Open** is a golf tournament that is part of the European Seniors Tour. Open to amateur and professional players. Tel: 422-4653 for further information.

Kensington Oval is awash with local and visiting cricket fans enjoying the annual **Test cricket series**, and the carnival atmosphere not uncommon at Caribbean sporting events.

May/June

Gospelfest, held during the latter part of May, is a weekend of gospel concerts featuring top local and international performers at venues across the island.

The **Barbados African-American Film Festival** features a selection of old and new films, seminars, a series of film workshops, and social gatherings for festival goers.

The **Barbados International Track & Field Classic** features top Barbadian and international sports stars.

In June the **Barbados Pan Festival** showcases steel pan music and musicians. The event culminates in a competition of the best in the region.

July/August

Crop Over, the island's biggest national festival, spreads over the entire month of July, culminating on the first Monday in August. This national celebration, one of the region's oldest festivals, heralded the end of the sugar crop and was traditionally characterised by feasting and dancing in the plantation yards *(see page 15)*.

Today Crop Over features a daily slate of cultural, historical, and musical events. Much interest is focused on calypso competitions that start in the 'tents' and progress through eliminations to the finals. On the last four days of the festival are the Pic-O-De-Crop Finals; Bridgetown Market (craft fair); Cohobbolo Pot, a variety show, and the road march and costumed parade on Grand Kadooment Day.

The **Banks Hockey Festival** attracts mens', womens' and mixed teams from around the world. For information, tel: Will Alleyne 426-0909.

October

Sun, Sea, and Slams International Bridge Festival is an annual five-day bridge competition held around the middle of the month.

November

The year's major **international surfing competition** is traditionally held in November. The premier surfing event, held at Bathsheba's 'soup bowl,' tests the mettle of top regional and North American talent.

National Independence Festival of Creative Arts (NIFCA) celebrates the island's independence with a month of displays and competitions in all facets of the creative arts such as dance, music, visual arts and crafts.

Barbados also celebrates independence with a program of community activities. Official Independence Day ceremonies normally take place at the Garrison Savannah.

December

Run Barbados is an annual international road race comprising two events, a (6-mile) 10-km race and a marathon. It is held in the first weekend in December.

Left: racing at the Garrison
Top: watching the Independence Day parade. **Right:** training for a road race

Practical
Information

GETTING THERE

Most visitors enter Barbados by air, unless they are passing through for the day on a cruise ship. The island has one airport, **Grantley Adams International**, at the south end of the island, which operates 24-hours and has one of the longest runways in the region. It has a small inbound duty-free shopping outlet and a Tourism Authority information booth in the arrivals hall.

A good taxi service operates from just outside the departure lounge. Fares are fixed according to the length of the journey and are posted on a board; be sure to check and agree on a price before you set out. There is also a bus stop nearby, at the airport terminal, for the adventurous or budget-conscious visitor who has traveled light.

Barbados is served by several international and regional air carriers. British West Indian Airways (BWIA) International flies a regular service between Barbados and several North American and European destinations, including Miami, New York, and London. Air Jamaica operates flights to Miami, Atlanta, Baltimore, Boston, Chicago, Florida, Houston, Newark, Philadelphia, and Los Angeles via Montego Bay.

American Airlines operates daily between Barbados and Puerto Rico, Miami, and New York. US Airways also have a service to the island, and Air Canada flies direct from Montreal and Toronto.

British Airways and Virgin Atlantic Airways have regular flights into Barbados from the UK. Other European destinations are serviced by Condor via Frankfurt.

South America connects to Barbados via Suriname Airways and the inter-island carrier LIAT (Leeward Island Air Transport). Along with LIAT and Caribbean Airlines, several regional charters link Barbados to other Caribbean islands. Several charters fly to Barbados from European and North American destinations in the winter.

Left: at the heliport
Right: taking a sea bath

Barbados is a primary port of call in the Caribbean and several cruise lines make day stops year round. The large cruise ship terminal at Deep Water Harbour is about one mile (1.6 km) from Bridgetown. There are shopping and banking facilities, and taxis are usually available when a ship is in port.

TRAVEL ESSENTIALS

Passports/Visas

Everyone entering Barbados should hold a valid passport and a return ticket. Make sure you know with whom and where you are staying in Barbados, as you are likely to be asked by immigration officers.

Visas are required for all people traveling from Eastern European nations, most Asian and Arab countries, the People's Republic of China, Taiwan, India, Pakistan, non-Commonwealth countries of Africa, Guatemala, Honduras, Haiti, and all South American countries except Argentina, Brazil, Colombia, and Venezuela.

Check the travel and entry requirements at your nearest consulate office or your travel agent, because the visa list is subject to change, or visit www.foreign.gov.bb for visitor information.

Vaccinations

Vaccinations and a certificate of proof are required for travelers from infected areas only. However, it is always advisable to ensure that your tetanus is up to date.

Customs

Customs may ask you to open your luggage for a search, which is not uncommon. Most customs officers are pleasant and reasonable, and after a quick look, will send you on your way.

Customs limits are 200 cigarettes or 50 cigars, and 1 liter of spirits.

Barbados frowns on the importation of plant matter, fresh produce, and certain other unprocessed perishable goods. If you must bring something of this nature, check with the nearest Barbados Consulate or tourism office on the current regulations. When you arrive there is an agriculture counter in the terminal where these items are examined.

Drug smuggling is a very serious offence, punishable with imprisonment, and sentences can be lengthy and severe.

Pets

Barbados is one of a handful of rabies-free nations. Importation of any rabies-prone pet from anywhere in the world (other than England) must first go through a six-month quarantine in the United Kingdom. For details, tel: 427-5073.

Climate

Barbados has a consistent year-round tropical climate, with temperatures averaging 84–88°F (29–31°C) during the day and 75–79°F (24–26°C) at night. Trade winds cool the island most of the year.

While the island enjoys some 3,000 hours of sun annually, June to November is the official hurricane (rainy) season. The first few months usually bring little more than the occasional rainy spell, but in September and October storm activity in the region is at a peak. Barbados has not had a direct hit by a hurricane since 1955, but weather systems that bring days of rain are most frequent during this period.

The dry season is December to June, when, except for sudden sharp showers that quickly pass, the sun reigns.

Clothing

Barbados is a tropical climate, so humidity is higher than in temperate zones.

With temperatures around 30°C and high humidity, especially between May and October, it can be a little uncomfortable so bring lightweight, loose clothing made from cotton, linen, and other natural fabrics.

Casual apparel is fine for the day and most evenings. However, you should try to respect the local population by refraining from wearing beachwear and skimpy clothing in public places.

Evening wear can be dressy if you plan to dine in an upmarket restaurant or enjoy a floor show. Sports shirts for men and light dresses for women are acceptable. For the most part elegant attire is quite satisfactory, with very few formal occasions that require a jacket and tie. Most nightclubs do not allow men to wear hats or sleeveless shirts, and some do not allow shorts. Shoes and shirts are required in all public places.

During winter the night air can be cool so a light sweater or wrap is advisable.

Electricity

The electricity in Barbados is dependable and steady. Barbados operates on the odd system of 110 volts/50 cycles, but most 60 cycle items work here. The typical North American two-prong plug is used throughout the island and many hotels have 220 volt outlets in the bathrooms.

Right: schoolgirl at play

Time Zone

Barbados is in the United States Eastern Standard time zone, four hours behind Greenwich Mean Time. It does not operate Daylight Savings Time.

GETTING ACQUAINTED

Geography

Shaped something like a pear, Barbados is a mere 14 miles (22km) wide by 21 miles (34km) long. The most easterly of the Caribbean chain, this 166-sq-mile (429-sq-km) island is a relatively flat, coral-capped island compared to its volcanic neighbors. Though lacking the sharply crested terrain of the other islands, Barbados has a character all its own. The brisk, cosmopolitan texture of Bridgetown and other urban centers combines with the gentle charm of undulating greenery and colorful rows of quaint chattel house villages.

About one-sixth of the island, in the Scotland District in the northeast, is dramatically jagged with a terrain of clay and sedimentary deposits. Much of the pre-history of the island chain is readily visible in these rocky formations. The island's tallest point is 1,100-ft (336-m) Mount Hillaby in St Thomas, just north of the island center.

Government/Economy

Barbados enjoys one of the oldest parliamentary systems in the world (its first representative body was formed in 1639). Unlike other islands, it remained peacefully in the hands of the British until November 30, 1966, when it gained independence.

Barbados operates under a democratic parliamentary system, or a constitutional monarchy, with the island's Governor General representing the monarchy as head of state. The Senate and House of Assembly are headed by the Prime Minister. There are two principal political parties which represent 28 constituencies.

The economy is driven by sugar and tourism. For centuries sugar was the island's main revenue earner, but in the early 1980s tourism usurped it as the main foreign exchange earner. While winter is known as the high season for tourism, traditional patterns are changing due to the high number of budget travelers arriving on charter flights during the summer months. A strong offshore financial sector has helped diversify the economy making it one of the strongest and most stable in the Caribbean.

Population

Barbados is one of the most densely populated islands in the region, with some 280,000 inhabitants. More than 90 percent of the population is of African descent, with principal minority populations comprising Caucasian, East Indian, and Syrian/Lebanese.

Religion

More than 100 denominations and sects thrive, the largest being Anglican. Other religions include Baptist, Christian Science, Jewish, Methodist, Moravian, Muslim, Pentecostal, and Roman Catholic.

Language/Dialect

On first hearing locals talk, you may well ask if it is English they are speaking. It is. Bajan dialect is colorful and expressive, with many nuances and shortcuts. Most notable is the habit of clipping off the end consonant of words. 'Helping' verbs are rarely used in dialect, so instead of 'I have gone' or 'I will go' you will hear 'I gone.' The 'th' sound is generally clipped to either a 't' or 'd' sound, so 'that' becomes 'dat' and 'youth' become 'yute.' Pick up a copy of Frank Collymore's *Bajan Dialect* at local bookshops.

Right: at the barber shop

practical information

MONEY MATTERS

Currency

Barbados carries its own currency, the Barbados dollar, which is tied to the US dollar. The exchange rate is set at BDS $1.98 to US$1, and this is the rate (plus some fees) you will get in the banks and most stores. However, the street rate is a straight two to one, and it is not uncommon to mix currencies when dealing with ancillary services such as taxis.

Credit Cards

Major credit cards are readily accepted in restaurants, hotels, and most shops catering for visitors.

Banking

Banks usually require customers to show their passport and ticket when exchanging foreign currency in either direction. Local laws prevent Barbadians from obtaining foreign currency above a certain limit, so it is standard procedure to show these items, particularly if you are changing local money into your own currency. You may need a passport when getting cash advances on your credit card.

ATM machines that will dispense local currency against your credit and debit card are encountered island-wide. Virtually all these machines require a PIN (Personal Identification Number), without one you will have to exchange your money inside the bank. As a rule, bank hours are Monday to Thursday 8am–3pm and Friday 8am–5pm.

Tipping

Bajans love to be tipped. From the time you step into the arrivals hall and the porters (Red Caps) begin hounding you for your luggage, tips will be expected. Red Caps are entitled to BDS$1 per bag. People tend to tip higher, but if a Red Cap tries to insist on more, you needn't feel obliged to give it.

Check your bill carefully at restaurants to see if a service charge has been included. If not, a 10–15 percent tip is the norm.

Departure Tax

Departure tax is BDS$60, payable in cash, it is sometimes included in travel packages.

GETTING AROUND

By Bus

The cheapest, and certainly most elbow-rubbing, way to get around the island is by bus. The bus system is partially privatized, so the urban districts are flooded with a host of PSVs (public service vehicles). There are large government buses, squat yellow mini-buses, 'maxi taxis,' and small vans (ZM and ZR plates) all along the south and west coast stretches. There is a standard flat fare, but you must have the exact change on government buses.

For buzzing up and down your particular stretch of coast or popping into Bridgetown, any of the PSVs will do, and since there are so many of them your wait will be short. But because all transport emanates from Bridgetown, with little cross-country movement, travel in rural areas is time-consuming. It means a trip into Bridgetown, then walking the length of the city to change terminals and quite often a long wait before departure.

In the country, buses are rarely on time and waits at stops can be irritatingly long.

By Car

Renting a car offers greater independence than using public transport, and Barbados has more than 60 car hire companies offering everything from little convertible mini mokes to air-conditioned vans. Rates are flat and most of the rental agents will issue local licenses off your home license (US$5) along with delivery and 24-hour emergency service.

Although Barbados is small, driving on the **left** side of its meandering 900 miles

Left: downtown Bridgetown

(1,450km) or so of narrow roads is a challenge for some. Besides getting lost, which is a given, the 30mph (50kph) speed limit seems fast when learning to share the road with bicycles, donkey carts, pedestrians, and push carts laden with anything from 20-ft (6-m) boards to piles of chairs. Luxuries like pavements and verges are seen only on the few real highways, where speed limits are 50mph (80kpm).

The most important thing to remember when driving on Barbados is to stay alert and on the left. In the country, hug your side of the road and announce yourself at every corner by honking the horn.

Cars can be rented for about US$200–300 per week depending on the size and features of the vehicle. **Corbins Car Rentals** in Collymore Rock (tel: 427-9531) has one of the largest and most reliable fleets on the island. Prices are the same all year and you can drop the car off at the airport when you leave. **Stoutes Car Rental** in St Philip (tel: 416-4456) has a good fleet of sturdy vehicles, and **Top Car Rentals** also in Christ Church (tel: 435-0378) offers good service and reasonable year-round prices. In high season it is recommended that you book in advance as rental vehicles quickly become scarce.

By Taxi
Taxis are everywhere and, while pricey as a regular means of transport, are recommended at night if you are not renting your own vehicle or wish to try a restaurant outside your area and plan to consume alcohol. Rates are fixed by destination, but it is always advisable to agree on the fare before setting off.

By Bicycle/Motorbike
Be careful when considering bicycle or motorbike rental, as they can prove dangerous on roads with no verge, and some companies do not carry insurance.

HOURS & HOLIDAYS

Business Hours
Most stores are open from 8am–4pm on weekdays and on Saturday morning. The larger supermarkets usually stay open until 7pm or 8pm Monday to Saturday; the few that open on Sunday, do so only in the morning. Some minimarts and Bridgetown pharmacies also open on Sunday mornings. Many petrol stations, especially those along the busy south and west coast highways, have large 24-hour convenience stores.

Public Holidays
New Year's Day; Errol Barrow Day (January 21); Good Friday; Easter Monday; Heroes Day (April 28); May Day (May 1); Whit Monday (varies each year); Emancipation Day (August 1); Kadooment Day (first Monday of August); United Nations Day (first Monday of October); Independence Day (November 30); Christmas Day and Boxing Day (December 25 and 26).

BEACHES

Thanks to its coral base, Barbados is blessed with sandy white beaches and blue seas. There are long stretches of good beach as well as tucked-away coves nestling between rocky shorelines. While the island's beaches are superb, sea conditions can vary dramatically.

West & Atlantic Coasts
The west coast has mostly calm bathing ideal for swimming, sailing, parasailing, jet skiing, and scuba diving. Snorkelling is particularly good around the coral reefs.

Above: take extra care if you decide to tour by bicycle

A visit to the underwater park at **Folkstone Marine Park** just north of Holetown is a good place to see a wide variety of coral and tropical fish and to swim. To feed turtles head to Mount Standfast. Watch out for spiny 'cobblers' (black sea urchins) because touching or scraping their spines is very painful.

On occasions when there is a north swell surfing is popular at **Bat's Rock** in St Michael and **Duppy's** in St Lucy.

While most of the west coast, from Brighton to Speightstown, is packed with good beaches, among the best is **Paradise Beach** at the south end of St James. Though Paradise Hotel, which flanks the beach is closed, you can enjoy this lovely spot by the public access on the south end of the property.

Sandy Lane, where the island's five-star hotel stands, has a wonderful beach; public access is at the south end of the estate.

A little north of Holetown a road on the north side of the **Colony Club** offers public access to one of the best beaches, in front of the famous **Heron Bay House**, a wonderful, little-known stop.

Mullins Bay in St Peter, just in front of the restaurant, has a good beach, and **Heywoods Beach**, next to Almond Beach Village is also a good bet in the north. While the northern St Peter and St Lucy beaches are lovely to look at, the undertows and currents here are ferocious. In fact it is best not to swim anywhere along the Atlantic side of the island, because there are generally no lifeguards on duty. However, lifeguards are on

duty daily at **Barclays Park**, East Coast Road, **soup bowl** in Bathsheba (ideal for surfing not swimming), **Bath Beach** in St John, and **Crane Beach** in St Philip.

As with all beaches, but in particular the entire north and eastern Atlantic sides, never swim alone and always heed local warnings. What looks safe could prove treacherous.

South Coast

The south coast beaches are popular, with small waves ideal for body surfing, boogey boarding, swimming, sailing and windsurfing.

The beach at **Long Bay** can be accessed through Chancery Lane. Though a bit secluded, it is good for walks, and swimming is good too, but watch out for the strong currents. **Round Rock**, also called **Silver Rock Beach**, is a lovely wide beach in Silver Sands, excellent for windsurfing and kite sailing, but it also packs a powerful undertow. On the south coast before Oistins is **Enterprise** or **Miami Beach**, a fairly sheltered and popular beach with a lifeguard on duty.

At the south end of St Lawrence is **Dover Beach**, a popular spot with many facilities. **Accra** at **Rockley Beach Park**, is the island's most popular beach because it is wide and long and has excellent swimming, facilities, and a lifeguard. Near Bridgetown is large, sheltered **Carlisle Bay**, dotted with yachts and site of a sunken wreck. This calm bay is a favorite with locals and visitors alike.

ACCOMMODATION

If you are looking for a place to stay, Barbados has hundreds of choices. They range from the sophisticated luxury hotels and villas (US$400+ per night), mainly found on the west coast, to basic guesthouses and privately owned cottages. All-inclusive hotels are also popular. An accommodation listing can be found at Barbados Tourism Offices *(see page 91)*, www.barbados.org or the Barbados Hotel & Tourism Association, tel: 426-5041; www.bhta.org.

During the summer (late April–October), when rain is expected more frequently, you can expect a drop in prices compared to what you would pay in the winter months. The prices indicated here are based on a room

Top: fun at the beach

for two during high season (winter: November to April). Package deals through travel agents may give substantial savings.
$ = under US$100; $$ = US$100–150; $$$ = US$150–250; $$$$ = US$250 and above.

South Coast
The south coast is the favored area for value-for-money accommodation. Crammed with activity from Carlisle Bay to St Lawrence Gap, what this shore lacks in serenity it makes up for in convenience.

Large Hotels
Accra Beach Hotel
Worthing, Christ Church
Tel: 435-8920
www.accrabeachhotel.com
Large quiet complex on a popular beach, close to many amenities and Bridgetown. Popular with business travelers. $$$

Almond Casuarina Beach Club
St Lawrence Gap, Christ Church
Tel: 428-3600
www.almondresorts.com
Family friendly with facilities for kids and disabled guests; rooms with kitchenette; beautiful gardens and local art on display. $$$

Coconut Court Beach Hotel
Worthing, Christ Church
Tel: 427-1655
www.coconut-court.com
Young and lively, with recreational rooms and friendly staff. 60 rooms have been completely refurbished. Good value. $$

Gems of Barbados
The Savannah; Blue Horizon; Time Out
Tel: 435-9473
www.gemsbarbados.com
A chain of small hotels along the south coast in popular locations. $$–$$$

Grand Barbados Beach Resort
Aquatic Gap (off Bay Street), St Michael
Tel: 426-4000
www.grandbarbados.com
Rooms have a view across beautiful Carlisle Bay. Needs an update, but close to Bridgetown and popular with business travelers. $$$

Sandy Bay Beach Club
Worthing, Christ Church
Tel: 435-8000
www.sandybaybeachclub.com
All inclusive with pleasant rooms and suites; spectacular beach close to amenities. $$$

Small Hotels
Coral Mist Beach Hotel
Worthing, Christ Church
Tel: 435-7712
www.coralmistbarbados.com
Renovated hotel on the beach, with two pools, a gym, restaurant, and kitchenettes in all rooms. $$

Little Arches Hotel
Enterprise Beach Road, Christ Church
Tel: 420-4689
www.littlearches.com
Boutique hotel looking across to Miami Beach. Use of hotel yacht. $$$

Little Bay Hotel
St Lawrence Gap, Christ Church
Tel: 435-7246
www.littlebayhotelbarbados.com
Charming studios with kitchenettes; a good restaurant; close to the beach, shops, and nightclubs. Good value. $–$$

Long Beach Club Hotel
Chancery Lane, Christ Church
Tel: 428-6890
email: jdell@sunbeach.net
In a quiet, windswept spot on one of the longest beaches; near the airport. $

Apartments/Villas
Magic Isle Apartments
Rockley, Christ Church
Tel: 435-6760
www.magicislebarbados.com
Centrally located self-contained one- or two-bedroom apartments, balcony to sea. $$

Nautilus Beach Apartments
Bay Street, St Michael
Tel: 426-3541
www.nautilusbeach.com
Simple one-bedroom apartments with kitchenettes on a beautiful bay close to Bridgetown. $

Pirate's Inn
Hastings, Christ Church
Tel: 426-6273
www.pirates-inn.com
Studio apartments with kitchenettes near to beach. Good value. $

Sea Foam Haciendas
Worthing, Christ Church
Tel: 435-7380
www.seafoamhaciendas.com
Central, well-equipped kitchen, two-bedroom balcony apartments on Worthing Beach. Can be good value. $$–$$$

Guest Houses
Abbeville Hotel
Rockley, Christ Church
Tel : 435-7924
www.funbarbados.com
A good low-cost bet. Close to Accra Beach and amenities. $

Shell's Guest House
Worthing, Christ Church
Tel: 435-7253
www.shellsguest.com
Basic rooms, some with a shared bathroom. Near spectacular Sandy Beach. Small, excellent affordable restaurant. Gay friendly. $

Crystal Waters
Worthing, Christ Church
Tel: 435-7514
www.crystalwaters.com
Basic accommodation near Sandy Beach.

All-Inclusive Resorts
Packages include meals, drinks, and most, if not all on-site leisure and sporting activities.

Allamanda & Amaryllis Beach Resorts
Hastings, Christ Church
Tel: 427-2541 or 435-6694
Sister hotels with all-inclusive option. Both oceanfront properties have pools, restaurants, and some rooms with wheelchair access. $$$

Island Inn Hotel
Aquatic Gap (off Bay Street), St Michael
Tel: 436-6393
www.islandinnbarbados.com
Small, converted inn near to the sea and Bridgetown. Ideal for business travelers. $$–$$$

Turtle Beach Resort
Dover, Christ Church
Tel: 428-7131
www.eleganthotels.com
An attractive beachfront property with suites, child care facilities, three pools, Jaccuzi, tennis courts, gym, and water sports. $$$

West Coast
The west coast has the most upmarket hotels on the island. However, if you are on a budget, apartment hotels with your own cooking facilities are the way to go. Remember summer rates and package deals can make the luxury hotels more affordable.

Several property companies specialize in villa rentals: **Bajan Services**, tel: 422-2618, www.bajanservices.com; **Alleyne Aguilar & Altman Ltd**, tel: 432-0840, www.aaalt man.com; **Realtors Limited**, tel: 432-6930, www.realtorslimited.com.

Hotels
Cobbler's Cove
Road View, St Peter
Tel: 422-2291
Elegant beachfront hotel with luxurious suites and excellent restaurant. Friendly staff. $$$

Elegant Hotels Group
Tel: 432-6500
www.eleganthotels.com
A group of luxurious all-inclusive hotels along the west coast including: **Tamarind**

Top: picturesque Cobbler's Cove

Cove, Turtle Beach, Colony Club, Crystal Cove and **Coconut Creek**. $$$$

Sandridge Beach Hotel
St Peter
Tel: 422-2361
www.barbadostravel.com
A good hotel at a moderate price. $$

Apartments & Guest Houses
Claridge's Inn
Gibbes, St Peter
Tel: 422-2403
Guest house for the budget conscious. $

Homar Rentals
St James
Tel: 432-6750
www.barbadostraveler.com
One-, two- and three-bedroom apartments, close to beach. Young guests. Properties include: **Traveller's Palm, Halcyon Palm**. $–$$

Inn on the Beach
Holetown, St James
Tel: 432-0385
Family-run studios with kitchenette close to shops. $$

Little Good Harbour
Fort Rupert, Shermans, St Peter
Tel: 439-3000
www.littlegoodharbourbarbados.com
One-, two- and three-bedroom cottage apartments on a quiet bay. With the **Fish Pot** restaurant, known for its seafood. $$$

Smugglers' Cove
Paynes Bay, St James
Tel: 432-1741
www.barbados.org/hotels/smugglerscove
Only 20 units at this reserved property on a beautiful beach. $$

All-Inclusive Resorts
Almond Beach Club & Spa
Vauxhall (Sunset Crest), St James
Tel: 432-7840
www.almondresorts.com
An elegant adults-only all-inclusive resort with gym, water sports, spa facilities (pay extra). Close to shops and amenities. $$$

Almond Beach Village
Heywoods, St Peter
Tel: 422-4900
www.almondresorts.com
A family resort with golf, tennis, squash, gym, and watersports activities. $$$

Mango Bay
Holetown, St James
Tel: 432-1384
www.mangobaybarbados.com
Charming property with pool, close to popular nightlife. Friendly staff. $$$

The Regent St James
Holetown, St James
Tel: 432-6666
www.barbados.org/hotel/theregent
One-bedroom suites with ocean views. Near shops, restaurants, and amenities. $$$

East Coast and Beyond
This coast offers visitors a different perspective of Barbados. The pounding seas and fresh wind, and rugged coastline have made it a surfers' paradise and ideal for hiking. Its quaint coastal villages are home to real country folk. It is far from the capital and other attractions, so you will need to hire a car to explore it.

Hotels
Atlantis Hotel
Tent Bay, Bathsheba
Tel: 433-9445
Historic Barbadian hotel overlooking Tent Bay with basic, budget accommodation. Most noted for its delicious local cuisine at the Wednesday and Sunday buffet. $

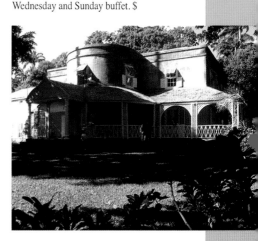

Right: Villa Nova

The Crane Resort & Residences
The Crane, St Philip
Tel: 423-6220
www.thecrane.com
Private residence resort built around an 18th-century mansion overlooking the Atlantic Ocean. Ongoing redevelopment work on the property is creating accommodation in five-story blocks (time-share), a health spa and a glass elevator, which will take guests from the main building on the cliff to the beach below. Luxurious suites with lovely ocean views and a clifftop pool; great pink sand beach. $$$

New Edgewater
Bathsheba, St Joseph
Tel: 433-9900
www.newedgewater.com
Small refurbished hotel with old-world rustic atmosphere and a breathtaking cliff-top view. Basic rooms, one luxury suite, swimming pool and good dining. For the budget-conscious traveler. Close to the surf of the Soup Bowl. $$

Round House
Bathsheba, St Joseph
Tel: 433-9678
www.funbarbados.com
Only a few rooms available, essentially a good restaurant with four rooms, which have an en suite shower. Ideal for a short quiet stay and close to good surfing. Excellent restaurant. Good value. $–$$

HEALTH

The standard of health facilities is relatively high in Barbados. There are two hospitals, Queen Elizabeth (QEH, government run) and Bayview (private). QEH is a 600-bed facility with several specialized services, an emergency room and a rather slow ambulance service. There are private ambulance services run by the Red Cross, Get Help and Island Care. AAA Air Ambulance and Aero Jet International Air Ambulance are for emergencies that can only be treated abroad.

The emergency department at QEH can be very busy and it is not unusual to have to wait for hours to be seen by a doctor. To avoid a long wait try FHM a 24-hour private emergency service on 3rd Avenue, Belleville in St Michael.

There are several polyclinics island-wide and a large number of private medical practitioners, dentists, and pharmacies. Most large hotels have a doctor on call or can refer you. Embassies also have a list of approved physicians and specialists who they will refer you to in case of an emergency.

Barbados has a decompression chamber for diving mishaps, operated by the Barbados Defence Force.

Medical insurance from recognized insurance plans is sometimes accepted at private facilities, but you should verify this in advance. The QEH does not, as a rule, accept overseas medical plans, nor does it take all credit cards.

PERSONAL SAFETY

Barbados is not a crime-prone destination, but, like anywhere else, crime does exist. Visitors often tend to relax usual personal safety precautions on vacation, and this is a mistake. Crime is generally opportunistic so always secure your valuables and be alert. Most hotels have house or room safes, so use them. Don't leave valuables unattended on the beach or in vehicles, especially in secluded spots.

Out on the road
If you are going to explore remote areas do so in a group rather than alone, or as a couple.

Top: the elegant pool at The Crane

Certain areas are not safe to walk alone or in small groups at night, so check with your hotel staff before setting off.

Barbadian vendors can seem quite aggressive sales people. It's always best to be polite, but if you are not interested a firm 'no thank you' with a smile should be enough.

Unofficial parking attendants and 'boys on the block' giving directions, often try to persuade visitors to tip them. This is not necessary, but it is a good idea to carry a local dollar coin or two for such events. Do not feel pressured to part with more cash.

Barbados does not have a serious drug problem, but like other countries their use has grown. Drugs are not tolerated, carrying even small quantities for personal use can result in a hefty fine and/ or imprisonment.

COMMUNICATIONS & NEWS

Newspapers

Barbados has two daily newspapers, *The Nation* and *The Advocate*, and a weekly newspaper, *The Broadstreet Journal*. The publications are updated daily and can be found on the internet provider websites: www.caribsurf.com and www.sunbeach.net. Two visitor publications come out every two weeks, *The Visitor* and *The Sunseeker*; the *Barbados Holiday Guide* is quarterly. All are free at most tourist outlets. There are a few annual visitor guides, *Barbados in a Nutshell*, which is free at many tourist centers. *The Ins and Outs of Barbados* and *Sporting Barbados* are often found free in guest rooms. Foreign publications are readily available throughout the island.

Television & Radio

There is one government-run television station, CBC (Caribbean Broadcasting Corporation), although most hotels have satellite dishes giving them access to North American programming. Subscription cable services are available locally.

There are nine radio stations. CBC operates two: 900AM and Liberty 98.1FM, popular with teenagers. Starcom Network also has a number of stations including: VOB (Voice of Barbados) 92.9, the number one station, Hot 95.3, Love 104.1 and Gospel 790AM. There are also privately run BBS 98.7FM, Mix 96.9 and Faith 102.1FM.

Postal Information

There are post offices in every parish. The island's main post office is on the edge of Bridgetown. Most hotels and tourist outlets carry stamps and postcards, and your hotel will most likely post mail on your behalf. You will also find bright red postal slots in guard walls, the sides of buildings and other strange locations. Rest assured they are cleared each day so your mail is safe.

Telephone & Internet

The country code is (**246**).

Barbados has a reliable, island-wide phone service operated by Cable and Wireless (tel: 800-804-2994). It is linked to the United States DDD (Direct Distance Dialing) system, so credit card calls can be made direct.

Coin-operated phone booths are located throughout the island. You can buy calling (phone) cards, which allow you to speak from any touch tone phone for as long as you like, at Cave Shepherd on Broad Street in Bridgetown and any Cable and Wireless location. They come in denominations of BDS$10, $20, $40 and $60. Business travelers can also utilize video conferencing facilities. Phone calls from hotels are expensive. Most of the larger hotels offer fax and email services.

Cellular phones can be used on the island but it might be cheaper to rent one or buy a Barbados SIM card for your handset. Mobile phone service is provided by Cable and Wireless and Digicel (tel: 434-3444).

Right: making a call

High-speed internet is widely available and there are at least three internet service providers on the island. Cyber cafés can be found in Bridgetown and the tourist hubs on the west and south coasts.

ATTRACTIONS

Cruising
Sail the Caribbean waters by day or night. A large number of boats are operated by Tall Ships (tel: 430-0900) such as the pirate boat *Jolly Roger*, which has fun daytime cruises, or the steamboat-style *MV Harbour Master*, which has day or evening cruises on four decks, with food and loud music to dance to. Private catamaran charters are available on *Cool Runnings* (tel: 436-0911) or on *Heat Wave* (tel: 429-9283). If you prefer a traditional vessel, sunset champagne cruises are offered by *Stiletto Cruises*, Dover, Christ Church; tel: 230-3495.

National Trust Walks
These are real treats, not just because they give you an opportunity to see the island in the company of knowledgeable guides, but also because they are free. Hike Barbados is a year-round Sunday activity with 6am and 3pm 5-mile (8-km) hikes at three speeds and distances; the leisurely stop 'n' stare (5–6 miles/8–10km), a medium pace (8–10 miles/13–16km), and the fast-paced grin and bear it (12–14 miles/19–23km). At full moon a moonlight hike starts at 5.30pm, don't forget to bring a torch. Contact the Barbados National Trust at tel: 436-9033.

SPORTS

Barbadians love sport and with the tropical climate a wide variety of sports can be enjoyed throughout the year. For an up-to-date list of sporting events and dates call the BTA, tel: 427-2623 or check the website at www.barbados.org.

Cricket
The first love is of course **Cricket**, the national sport, which is played everywhere during the season, on fields, backyards, beaches, and of course on cricket grounds.
International and regional cricket tours are held between February and May; games are played at historic Kensington Oval, Bridgetown. International School's Cricket Competitions are held during the summer months. The Cricket World Cup Final is to be played in Barbados in 2007. For more information call the Barbados Cricket Association, tel: 436-1397.

Ball Games
Popular team sports include **football** (soccer), basketball, volleyball, rugby, field hockey, and netball.
Tennis fans can find courts at a number of hotels. There are also private clubs and tennis centers, such as the Barbados Lawn Tennis Association at the Sir Garfield Sobers Complex, Club Rockley, and Oceanview Tennis Centre. Sugar Hill, in St James, has a court with a turf and sand surface.

Water Sports
There is an Olympic-size swimming pool at the **Aquatic Centre**.
Most of the waters around Barbados are safe to swim in, except on the north and east coasts where strong currents and undertows can be dangerous. **Snorkeling** and **scuba diving** are popular activities and there are several independent dive shops, and others that operate through hotels. There are opportunities for wreck diving, and offshore there are coral reefs, and even opportunities to swim with, and feed, endangered turtles.
For the less adventurous a trip aboard the **Atlantis Submarine** (tel: 436-8929) or on a glass bottom boat will provide a views of colorful marine life.

Top: waiting for a bite

Surfing is popular all year with breaks 10–20ft (3–6m) regularly around the island. Annual surf events include the International Open Surfing Competition and National Finals in November at the soup bowl in Bathsheba on the east coast.

Windsurfing and **Kite Surfing** is best on the south coast. International windsurfing competitions are held annually at Silver Sands in January.

Sailing regattas worth noting are the Mount Gay Regatta at Christmas and the Harris Paints Regatta in summer.

The Barbados Turf Club (tel: 426-3980) has a busy **horseracing** calendar of 20 race days a year, the highlight is the Sandy Lane Gold Cup on the first weekend in March. This offers the Caribbean's biggest purse and is a keenly contested 9-furlong invitational race attracting A-class horses from around the region. The event draws a huge crowd, and has a celebratory atmosphere, with much pomp and ceremony.

Golf is experiencing a renaissance, with several courses built in recent years. There are three major courses at Royal Westmoreland, Sandy Lane, and the Barbados Golf Club, which is the only public facility on the island. In addition there is a driving range and miniature golf at the Barbados Academy of Golf (tel: 420-7405). Open international tournaments are scheduled in the winter.

USEFUL NUMBERS

Emergencies
Police   211
Fire   311
Ambulance (QEH)   511
Queen Elizabeth Hospital (public), Martindale's Road, St Michael, tel: 436-6450
FMH Emergency Centre (private), 3rd Avenue Belleville, St Michael, tel: 228-6120
Bayview Hospital (private), St Paul's Avenue, Bayville, St Michael, tel: 436-5446

Credit Card and Travelers' Checks
American Express:
Lost or stolen cards: 800-327-1267
Travelers' checks: 800-221-7282
MasterCard: 800-307-7309
Visa: 800-847-2911

Embassies and Consulates
Australia: Australian High Commission, Bishop's Court Hill, St Michael, tel: 435-2834
Canada: Canadian High Commission, Bishop's Court Hill, St Michael, tel: 429-3550
United Kingdom: British High Commission, Lower Collymore Rock, St Michael, tel: 430-7800
United States: Embassy of the United States, Bridgetown, tel: 436-4950

BARBADOS TOURISM AUTHORITY OFFICES

In Barbados
Harbour Road, St Michael, tel: 427-2623. There is also a BTA booth at the airport, or see website: www.barbados.org

Abroad
Canada
105 Adelaide Street West, Suite 1010, Toronto M5H 1PN, tel: 800-268-9122; 416-214-9880
4800 de Maisonneuve W, Suite 532, Montreal, Quebec H3Z 1M2, tel: 514-932-3206
United States
800 Second Avenue, New York, NY 10017, tel: 800-221-9831; 212-986-6516
3440 Wilshire Boulevard, Suite 1215, Los Angeles, CA 90010, tel: 213-380-2198
United Kingdom
263 Tottenham Court Road, London W1P 7LA, tel: (0) 20-7636-9448/9

FURTHER READING

Insight Guide: Barbados, Apa Publications edited by Caroline Radula-Scott, 2007.
A to Z of Barbadian Heritage (multiple authors), Jamaica, Heinemann Publishers (Caribbean Ltd), 1990
The Barbados Garrison and its Buildings, Warren Alleyne & Jill Sheppard, London, Macmillan Publishers Ltd 1990.
The Barbadian Rum Shop, Peter Laurie, Macmillan Publishers, Caribbean, 2001.
Ministry of Foreign Affairs website www.foreign.gov.bb

ACKNOWLEDGEMENTS

Photography

15T	**Tony Arruza**
10, 11, 13	**Barbados Museum & Historical Society**
12T	**Courtesy of Jamaica National Library**
1, 2/3, 5, 6/7, 15B, 20, 23T, 24, 25T&B, *26B, 27, 32, 33B, 35T, 36, 37T, 39T,* *42, 48, 49, 50, 51B, 53B, 54, 55T&B, 56,* *58, 61, 62, 63T, 64T&B, 65, 67, 68T&B,* *69, 70, 72, 74, 75, 77T&B, 78, 79, 81, 82,* *83, 86,87, 90*	**Martin Rosefeldt/Apa**
14	**Stephen Smith**
12B, 16, 21, 23B, 26T, 29T&B, 30T&B, 31 *33T, 37B, 39B, 40, 41, 43, 44, 45T&B, 46,* *47, 51T, 53T, 57T&B, 59T&B, 64T, 66, 71,* *76, 80, 84, 88, 89*	**Bill Wassman/Apa**
Front Cover	**Robert Harding Picture Library**
Back Cover	**Martin Rosefeldt/Apa,** **Bill Wassman/Apa**
Cartography	**Berndtson & Berndtson** **Maria Randell**

INDEX

OVER 250 DESTINATIONS IN 14 LANGUAGES

Let us be your guide

Your first visit – or a familiar destination? A short stay – or an extended exploration? Whatever your needs, there's an Insight Guide in a format to suit you. From Alaska to Zanzibar, we'll help you discover your world with great pictures, insightful text, easy-to-use maps, and invaluable advice.